The Fully Integrated Engineer

T0327345

The Fully Integrated Engineer

Combining Technical Ability and Leadership Prowess

Steven T. Cerri
Steven T. Cerri International
STCerri International

IEEE PCS Professional Engineering Communication Series

IEEE PRESS

WILEY

Library of Congress Cataloging-in-Publication Data is available.

ISBN: 978-1-118-85431-0

10 9 8 7 6 5 4 3 2 1

To McKenzie,
whom I am so proud of
as she creates her own message in the world.

Contents

Foreword

I've been privileged enough to have been asked to write forewords to a number of books, but I've never been as excited to write a foreword before as I am in writing this one.

First of all, Steven is both a personal friend and a professional colleague of mine, so while I may be biased, in my personal and professional opinion, Steven is a gem. He has unbending integrity and outstanding skills, making him one of the most effective, efficient, and empathetic change agents I've ever seen or worked with in a room of professionals.

My work is centered around the art of change with individuals and organizations. For more than two decades, one of my main areas of focus has been what I call "the personal side of change" in large multinational organizations, as well as in numerous technical fast growth start-ups and more than a few entrepreneurial and family-held businesses around the world. This part of the change process, the personal side, is all about how you get people in the organization to buy into the change process, model and outcome, and furthermore, how to get everyone pulling together in the same direction to take the action necessary to create the intended results.

Regardless of how powerful the strategy and plan of action are for making changes happen in organizations, without the team that needs to implement them working together and taking the appropriate action nothing happens, or worst the organization devolves instead of evolving as planned. This same effect can be seen when trying to develop and launch a new product, or when trying to merge two organizations together, or even in just managing an existing product for maximum return on investment or growth. The team that's responsible for the outcome must do what's necessary to succeed.

The process we use to insure that the kind of successes I refer to above are realized is called *management*. This is where I have a problem with Steven's book, despite my great sense of pleasure in reading it and honor in being asked to write this foreword.

Steven has aimed his book at engineers and technical professionals who are transitioning from being in technical roles to becoming professional managers. In this regard, his book is outstanding on every level; that's not what my challenge with his book is about in any way, shape, or form.

My challenge is that Steven's book may get lost on every other manager and leader in the organization because they may think what he writes about here is only for engineers and technical managers. However, it can and will help them if they read it!

In fact, this may be the best book I've ever read about how to address the personal side of business, which is the skill set every manager and leader in any organization needs to succeed. It isn't possible to move an organization forward at the current pace of the world without being able to connect with, communicate with, and move people ... and that's exactly what makes this book such a powerful resource.

Steven's book is a fundamental work on how people operate at the level of the beliefs and values that drive their action ... or lead to inaction. He has created a framework he calls, "personal behavioral subroutines" that defines how people get from data in the environment to the actions they take, or not. Then he translates this into a complete program on how to access one's own personal behavioral subroutines, as well as those of others, and step into the space of reorganizing them for success.

He's laid out this material in a series of short chapters with diagrams, explanations, exercises, and examples such that his book reads like a technical training manual for running the behaviors that lead to success in management, but at a level that makes the material remarkably accessible and easy to read, while also making it enjoyable to read. The diagrams alone are worth 10 times the cost of this book, and along with the text will make getting and absorbing what Steven's written, even the most technical concepts he's covered, an absolute walk in the park.

As an author of multiple books I know that this is no mean feat that Steven's accomplished, and hence my pleasure at writing this foreword. Simply put, this book should be in the hands of every organizational leader, manager or would-be manager ... and not on their shelf as some like to say. Instead, I recommend you keep it handy to pick up and review whenever you are unsure of what to do in a situation where you need to lead or guide others to creating outstanding outcomes. Leave it on the corner of your desk or the corner of your nightstand so you can access it at a moment's notice, I think it's both that relevant and that good, that once you've read it yourself you'll be forced to agree with my opinion.

As I said, I'm biased about Steven and his work. I personally know that this book represents the thinking of decades from one of the best minds I've ever encountered on the process of how to develop people in becoming world-class managers. While his record speaks for itself, this book gathers years of observation and insight on the art of management from Steven in a way that surpassed even my high expectation for what it would be before I read it.

I know as a reader, whether you truly are an engineer or a technical professional in a technical role, someone in any role in an organization moving up to a management position for the first time or a seasoned organizational leader or manager with many years of experience behind you already, what you glean from Steven's book from the first reading will be worth hundreds of times the amount of investment in time, energy, and money you put into it. In the next dozen or so readings, what you'll find yourself coming back to will likely make this one of the most valuable business books you'll ever come across or own.

In closing, I have just one final comment: plan on getting more than one copy if you're even thinking about loaning out to anyone, because once you do, you're going to have a very hard time getting it back.

Joseph Riggio, Ph.D.
Founder and President of Applied Behavioral Technologies, Inc.
Princeton, NJ

A Note from the Series Editor

With Steven T. Cerri's *The Fully Integrated Engineer: Combining Technical Ability and Leadership Prowess*, the IEEE Professional Communication Society (PCS), with Wiley-IEEE Press, continues its book series that aims to help engineering practitioners, instructors, and students alike with their technical communication efforts as they impact engineering work. However, *any* manager or project leader will certainly find gems of wisdom in this book, enabling active, positive change in workplace or classroom settings.

In my daily work, I have the privilege to see how engineering undergraduates, graduates, and practicing professionals (all levels) do their work. What intrigued me about Cerri's approach to retooling engineering practice was how spot on he was with the limiting actions that hold engineers back. He sees clearly how years and years of being a good student doesn't necessarily translate into being a good team player in a technical atmosphere beyond school. The breakthrough is how he asks people to recraft their approaches, acknowledging that shifting those old practices can be uncomfortable, and showing people how to methodically overhaul problem areas toward a fresh, collaborative, and productive work life.

Cerri's book combines the best of his many career talents: a career of engineering, an ability to see how engineering work gets done (or not done), and the patience and insight to help others move forward with their work and the satisfaction it can provide. Bringing all of these into alignment, Cerri's book is about good management skills, great communication skills (internal and external, for you have to communicate honestly with yourself before you can communicate well with others), and modes of action in the workplace that bring practitioners closer to solid engineering work.

The series has a mandate to explore areas of communication practices and application as applied to the engineering, technical, and scientific professions. Including the realms of business, governmental agencies, academia, and other areas, this series has and will continue to develop perspectives about the state of communication issues and potential solutions when at all possible.

All of the books in the fast-growing PEC series keep a steady eye on the applicable while acknowledging the contributions that analysis, research, and theory can provide to these efforts. There is a strong commitment from the Professional Communication Society of IEEE and Wiley to produce a set of information and resources that can be carried directly into engineering firms, technology organizations, and academia alike.

For the series, we work with this philosophy: at the core of engineering, science, and technical work are problem solving and discovery. These tasks require, at all levels, talented and agile communication practices. We need to effectively gather, vet, analyze, synthesize, control, and produce communication pieces in order for any meaningful work to get done. Cerri's insights helps move that mandate forward, and we welcome his contribution to the series.

Traci Nathans-Kelly, Ph.D.

Preface

You are an engineer. You believe you are a good engineer. You received good grades in college. You know how to solve technical engineering problems. You have recently joined the workforce. You are ready to go, and you are convinced you are going to show everyone just how good you really are.

Or…

You have been an engineer for a while. You really like your work but you are being passed over for advancement for lead positions. Others are being promoted and you are told you are not quite ready, but that doesn't make sense to you. You have experience. You have been in the company longer than those who are being promoted instead of you. What is wrong with this picture?

Or…

You have been a lead engineer for a while. A portion of your time you spend performing engineering technical work as an individual contributor and part of your time you spend performing management/lead tasks. You think you are doing well, but when you and your team completed your last project, you were returned to full-time individual contributor technical work. You are no longer a lead. Did you do something wrong? Was this a demotion?

Or…

You are an engineering student and you want to know what to expect once you enter the work environment. You want to know what it will take to be successful once you land that engineering job.

Or maybe…

You are a manager and some of your employees seem to be stuck in a set of behaviors that keep them from contributing to the team in effective ways. Other engineers don't particularly enjoy working with them. They are smart but often work as loners. As their manager, you would like to understand what is holding them back and what you can do to assist them in moving from being purely technical to being a full contributor to the team and maybe even into management.

If any of the above scenarios describe you, then this book is just for you. Throughout my career as an engineer, scientist, manager, and leader, it has become evident that there is a set of thinking processes and behaviors that makes good engineers very good engineers. These are the thinking processes and behaviors that engineering schools teach. However, these so-called "good engineer thinking processes and behaviors" do not necessarily make you a good team member or contributor or a good lead or a good manager.

I wrote this book because I saw—over and over again—engineers who thought that once they joined an organization, all they had to do to be successful was solve technical problems. They thought that all the organization wanted was their ability to bring engineering and technical solutions to bear. This is just not true. Organizations want more than just your ability to solve technical problems. They want you to be able to work well with others, to be a contributor on a team, to be able to control your behaviors and interact with others so that the team functions smoothly and effectively.

I wrote this book to give you the solutions to the misperception that what makes you a good engineer is sufficient to make you a good engineering employee.

This book describes, in detail, 15 thinking processes and behaviors that make engineers very good engineers. At the same time, these 15 behaviors make good engineers terrible team players, terrible contributors of ideas, and terrible leads and managers.

In this book, I list, describe, and unpack the 15 thought processes and behaviors that make you a good engineer and the 15 counter thought processes and behaviors that must be added to your repertoire in order for you to still be a good engineer while contributing to your team as a leader and manager.

This book is about making a transition from a very good engineer to a complete, fully contributing engineer. It is about making the transition from being a very good engineer to a fully effective lead and manager. I hope that my insights will teach you the skills not learned in college that are critical to your long-term success.

College taught you how to be a successful technical problem-solver. It probably did not teach you how to communicate well with others, or how to lead others, or how to get out of your own way.

In fact, I can't imagine an engineer or technical lead or manager for whom this book is not a perfect fit.

Enjoy!

Steven T. Cerri

Acknowledgments

This book is the culmination of a great deal of effort and input, and thanks are due to a variety of people and organizations.

Thanks go first to those who have made this publication possible. To begin I want to thank Wiley-IEEE Press for embarking on the path of producing a series of books to assist engineers in including in their careers more than engineering. In order to contribute engineering and technical knowledge to the betterment of humanity, more than just technical knowledge is necessary. To that end, Wiley-IEEE Press has developed an engineering and technical communication book series that focuses on providing just such knowledge; knowledge that is not generally taught in engineering curricula and yet, is essential for the successful engineering career. I owe thanks to Mary Hatcher, an original advocate of Wiley-IEEE Press, for initially reaching out to me to offer me this opportunity.

As part of the Wiley-IEEE Press I want to sincerely thank Traci Nathans-Kelly, my editor. Probably no one has ever been better at nudging me along without making me feel nudged. She is very good at what she does. And she allowed me to speak with my voice while at the same time ensuring that I spoke well.

Finally, this book is the culmination of one aspect of my career path and my life. This book is not the result of my interest in a topic and my commitment to conducting research on that topic and then writing a book on what I learned about that topic. There is no formal research in this book. There is only my life, my experience. And to that end, there are many who have contributed to what you will read in the chapters that follow because they have been an integral part and contribution to the experience of my life.

As is the case with most of us, my experience and therefore my career, begins with my family. At ten years old I became interested in rockets. My mother, Adele, would make trips to cigar stores to purchase expensive cigars in aluminum tubes. My father smoked the cigars and I used the aluminum tubes for the shell for my first zinc and sulfur propellant rockets. My father, Ivan, ensured that as my rockets grew in size, weight, and power, the machining and welding necessary were performed professionally at a machine shop, done to my specifications without me having to see a bill for the work. All I knew was that the machinists who worked there would chuckle as an eleven-year-old kid told them what he wanted them to do. And then there was my uncle, Joe, who ten years my elder, was my older brother, surrogate father, and helper in all those things a boy can't go to his parents for. He watched and encouraged me as I dreamt of traveling into space. These three people applauded and supported my choices, without questioning or judging what I wanted to do. Their support ultimately has led to this book. Thank you.

Engineering should not be a basket of knowledge or a toolbox filled with mathematical, scientific, and engineering tools. Engineering is not merely knowledge. Rather, engineering is a way of thinking. The person who taught me most powerfully to think like an engineer was Professor Alfred E. Andreoli, my fluid dynamics and thermodynamics professor at Cal Poly, San Luis Obispo. By example, by modeling the thought processes he used when he was instructing us, he taught me how to think not just how to know.

Once out of college, as a young engineer, there were two senior engineers and a manager who mentored me and set me on my path to management, leadership, and ultimately the information you find in this book. Tom Logsdon taught me how to be creative with ideas and how to let my mind wander off in order to create. From Tom I learned that any idea was worthy of sunlight. Phillip Harding taught me how to be a good person while enjoying engineering and art and life; and he taught me how to argue powerfully for my position. And Sam Garcia; the Spaniard who left home after high school and sailed on a merchant ship for two years before going to college. Sam taught me how common sense can often outweigh technical information. Sam also taught me how managers think and how to take responsibility for my own work. These three men were critical to my first getting a glimpse of the fact that good engineering is more than just having the right answer to a technical question.

I also am indebted to Susan Ackerman, without whose help and guidance this book would not exist. She taught me the fundamentals of Neruo-Linguistic Programming, which changed my life. Her wisdom, toughness, and gentleness were just what I needed and what she taught me set my career on an expanded pathway.

I owe much to Dr. Joseph Riggio, who is my friend and my teacher. He is a master of change work, of which I only scratch the surface in this book. There are people who intersect our lives and things are never the same. First they become our teachers and then they become our friends. Joe is one of those people, and the magic is that I can never tell when Joe is being my friend and when he is being my teacher.

I owe thanks to Dr. Gary Hansen, past dean of the Technology Management Program (TMP) in the Engineering Department of the University of California, Santa Barbara, California. Dr. Hansen gave me an opportunity to teach my material to a multidisciplinary group of undergraduate and graduate students in the TMP and it was one of the highlights of my career. Some of the material I taught is in this book. While the processes I present in this book were refined over the years as a manager and trainer and consultant, teaching at UCSB allowed me to fully apply these processes to students from a wide variety of disciplines and majors and to see that it works. It works very well, indeed.

I want to thank Christine Testolini-Kopec who always encouraged me while expressing mild surprise when this book became more than just my wistful musings.

Finally, to have a daughter with whom a parent can discuss their life's work as if they are talking to a peer is truly a gift. McKenzie is such a gift. Thank you, McKenzie, for our discussions and your ideas and for being a sounding board for me. You may not have known it when our discussions were occurring or when I watched you present your ideas to me and to others, but you have truly been a gift to me.

There are many, many more people who have helped me along my path and whose efforts have been instrumental in helping me to produce this book. They have been part of my journey on this topic to this point. Thank you. Thank you all.

1

What You Learned in College Is Limiting Your Growth As a Technology Professional

If you are an engineer, scientist, or technologist, at some point in your career, you will realize that what you learned in college is not enough to establish a successful, long-term career. Advancing your career, whether you want to remain technically focused or you want to become a manager, demands that you take off the technology blinders and give up the habits that you perfected as a technologist.

The typical path for engineers, scientists, and technologists once they leave school and enter the workforce is as follows. You begin your career as a technical *individual contributor*. You focus on your own individual contributions and you do your best to do a good job.

If you are successful as an individual contributor, often, you are given additional responsibilities, perhaps as a team lead or project manager of a small project. At some point, after having been given this additional responsibility, you realize that you are not as successful as you thought you would be. People do not listen to your directions, your project schedules slip, your meetings are difficult and ineffective, and you are stressed. Plus, you are not doing nearly as much technical work as you were doing before your "promotion." You begin thinking, "Just let me get back to my engineering work. That used to be so much more fun."

This situation is often the result of believing that what you learned as an engineer will also make you a good and successful manager or leader or long-term technologist.

The Fully Integrated Engineer: Combining Technical Ability and Leadership Prowess, First Edition. Steven T. Cerri.
© 2016 The Institute of Electrical and Electronics Engineers, Inc. Published 2016 by John Wiley & Sons, Inc.

You assume that the behaviors that made you a successful individual contributor will also make you successful as your career advances. They will not.

The first step in getting out of this fix and moving to success is to understand that there is something missing from your current abilities, and, therefore, something needs to be added. You need to make a shift. In order to make this shift, you must understand what you are doing now and what you need to add in order to change your behavior. This book will provide you with that information. It will highlight behaviors that make you a good engineer but will keep you from being successful long-term in related endeavors. It will also provide you with insights into what new beliefs and attitudes you need to add in order to be successful long-term.

When you were trained to be a successful engineer, scientist, or technologist, you learned to look and pay attention to hard, quantifiable, unambiguous, and repeatable data that you generated, analyzed, and counted on to do your work. This is what school taught you and this is what it means to be a competent engineer, scientist, or technologist.

But, as your career grows, you need to grow, too. If you want to be someone who can fully contribute to a team, who can manage projects and others, and who can lead a team or organization, the information that you will have available will often be, at best, fuzzy and less than ideal. In fact, in the non-technical world of effective communication, contribution, management, and leadership, there is often no way to turn that fuzzy, unreliable, and less than adequate data and information into clear, reliable and sufficient data that can lead to certainty in decision-making.

Successful engineers are looking for reliable, unambiguous, quantifiable data. Successful team contributors, leaders, and technical managers know they have (at best) fuzzy, unreliable data. The world of the engineer is built on certainty. The world of the long-term engineer, the manager or leader, is built on the understanding that some decision must be made with a level of uncertainty.

The role of engineers is to build the product, or to solve the problem, based upon quantifiable parameters and data. On the other hand, the role of technical managers or leaders is to drive the organization they lead into an unknown future and to bring together the resources at their disposal/command even when that outcome may seem unreasonable or unreachable to others.

Most engineers believe they can count on improving and perfecting their skills and advancing their careers by taking one step after another, doing what they were taught in school. They believe advancement is a logical step-by-step process into the future.

However, advancing your career represents a broadening of perspective and often involves a **phase shift** in your thinking. And that phase shift is a shift to embrace ambiguity and the lack of a precise, right answer to all questions and problems. It will require making decisions without as much "real" data as you would like. In a nutshell, it will require the application of judgment.

In fact, as an individual technical contributor, you are paid for providing the "right" answer. As a long-term technologist, or manager, or leader, you are paid for the application of your judgment when there is no "right" answer but only answers that work, some better than others.

This Book Is Your Safety Net

Even the best performers learn to fly using a safety net. The best safety net is not someone who has observed what you are going through from the sidelines. The best safety net is someone who has lived what you are living, right now.

I began my career as an aerospace engineer, with a Bachelor of Science in aeronautical engineering, advanced through geology to a Master's Degree in geophysics, and an Masters of Business Administration, and then became a technical manager, a systems engineer, and general manager of a division of a large software company. I have worked in the aerospace industry and the geophysical industry. I have worked for the US government, the Department of Defense, as well as a commercial printer company. As someone who has worked through the issues of being a technologist in the role of technical manager and leader, I know that it is not an easy world to navigate. It is more like a satellite traversing an asteroid field.

Everyone who wants to be a professional at some point in their career needs a safety net. And this book is one of your possible safety nets. It can help you understand where the surprises are, where the difficulties will occur, and where to find the dark and light corners. It can help to traverse to the other side, to the clearing, where your decisions move the team and the project forward smoothly and effectively.

This book will bring the safety net of my experience to teach you how to make the necessary changes on your own in the shortest amount of time and in the most elegant way possible. Depending on where you are in your career and what you want, different chapters of this book will appeal to you more or less. Take what you can use. Leave the rest for later.

2

Why Should You Read a Book by Me? Or ... Why Is This Book Important Now?

It is reasonable to ask, "Who is this guy and why should I read his book?"

Let me start by where I come from so that you can see how I so easily understand where the technical professional lives and what has to happen in order to achieve long-term career success and even to transition to management.

From the time I was a small boy, I knew I wanted to be an aeronautical/aerospace engineer. In elementary and high school, as well as in college, I built rockets. Not the cardboard kind, but rockets made of cold rolled steel tubing, using zinc and sulfur as solid propellant. My rockets reached altitudes of almost a mile and returned by parachute, sometimes. Although my friends helped me launch my rockets on launch day, I did most of my rocket work alone. I was not a member of a rocket society or club. I built my rockets through long hours in the family basement and launched them on our large family farm. I loved what I did and there was no need to share it with anyone else until the launch day.

I went off to college and received a Bachelor of Science degree in aeronautical engineering and upon graduation joined Rockwell International working in the advanced systems division as a flight performance engineer. After two years at Rockwell, I left to go back to school and received a Master of Science degree in geophysics. I then worked for several years for the United States Geological Survey as a software engineer and earth resources sciences researcher.

I then returned to Rockwell International to my flight performance team and worked on advanced deep space systems as a flight performance engineer and as chief systems

The Fully Integrated Engineer: Combining Technical Ability and Leadership Prowess, First Edition. Steven T. Cerri.
© 2016 The Institute of Electrical and Electronics Engineers, Inc. Published 2016 by John Wiley & Sons, Inc.

engineer. While at Rockwell, I met three other engineers and after several more years at Rockwell the four of us left and started our own company focused on software development and computer systems engineering.

After ten years and a couple of moves to field offices, the company was worth $100 million. During that time I received an M.B.A. Also, during that time I advanced my career from engineer to Program Manager, to Director of Engineering, to Vice President of Engineering, to Chief Operations Officer, to General Manager of a company division.

I later joined a start-up that became a highly successful commercial bar-code printer manufacturer. I was its first Product Manager and later became the Director of Corporate Training.

About 16 years ago, I started my own training, facilitation, coaching, and consulting company. It became clear that throughout my career I had developed a technology, processes, and an approach that most effectively transformed engineers and other technical professionals into even more effective technical professionals. That process transformed them into great technical managers, as well. I did not receive any official training in communication or management that was worth a dime along the way. All of the management training available then (and seemingly now as well), is most concentrated on using software to manage projects or on developing budgets and schedules. Even so-called communication and management courses are seldom taught by people who have communication or management experience in technical organizations. Instructors seldom have degrees in engineering or other technical fields (they often have degrees in psychology, not engineering) and often merely repeat what they have been told to say in their trainings. Nowhere was there anyone from the technical world who could teach me how to deal with people, and I quickly learned that dealing with people is what effective communication and good management are all about.

I learned how to deal with people on my own, often by taking courses that had nothing to do with technical management, and I became very, very good at interpersonal communication, management, leadership, and motivation. I built incredibly effective teams made up of people that other managers often did not want. I was able to turn around projects that had become unmanageable. I had a reputation of being able to handle very challenging issues around technology and people. Often, I was given the teams and projects that were broken, and I fixed them.

The processes and the technology of management that I developed over this period I call becoming a Fully Integrated Technical Professional©. It means being an engineer AND being able to contribute fully to your organization, using all your talents and all your capabilities. Whether you want to become a more effective engineer or you want to be an effective technical manager, I believe the processes I teach are necessary and, if followed, will get you there.

Since becoming a coach, facilitator/trainer, consultant, author, and speaker on this topic, I have worked with both large and small high-technology companies. I have been an adjunct professor at the University of California, Santa Barbara in the Technology Management Program in the Department of the Engineering. I have worked internationally training and coaching engineers, technologists and non-technologists to be more effective communicators and to smoothly transition to management.

Therefore, the reason I can write this book is because I have made the transition from engineer and scientist to manager myself and in the process I have developed tools that are unique and are tailored for the engineer by an engineer. I know what it takes to embrace this new career called *management*. I know what it feels like to be in the early stages of a technical management career. I know what it is like to think you have the skills to manage and yet have the feeling of uncertainty in the pit of your stomach when you approach a new management situation for the first time. I know what it is like to be in the cycle where you need to be a manager to get management experience and yet if you had the management experience you could be a manager.

I have coached many engineers into management positions and I am very proud of that fact. In addition, I have coached a handful of engineers who were just weeks away from employment termination when their managers contacted me. These engineers were going to be let go because they "just did not fit." No one argued that the engineers at risk of lay off were not smart engineers; indeed they were. But they either did not fit the organization or they failed in their first management attempts. They were slated for termination and I was their company's last resort in their attempt to keep these people at the company. They are now very successful senior engineers and managers in their organizations and I am very pleased to have played a role in their success.

You will note that there are few references in this book. I have not quoted other people or other sources. The reason for this is that if I have not used the tools, techniques, skills, and processes I put forth in these pages, and if I have not used them successfully, you will not hear about them. None of what you will find here is based on theories or present day fads. Everything I am sharing with you here has been applied by me, successfully, over and over and over again.

A Few Words in Praise of Steven T. Cerri's Work

I have taken a training course from Steven and I have had him as a coach and he is unique in both areas. Not only does Steven understand the world of the engineer, scientist, and technologist, but he also understands the worlds of managers and leaders. This combination makes him unique when it comes to his ability to merge different disciplines and to understand just what technical people need in order to become more effective and successful.

Steven is also refreshing in that he does not deal in theories. He deals in things that work and can be applied now. One of the most valuable aspects of Steven's trainings and coaching is that you get concrete, immediately applicable tools. As Steven often says, "If I haven't used what I'm teaching you successfully myself, you won't hear about it."

Ba Nguyen
Manager, QVS Engineering, a Premier Medical Device Company

* * *

The Fully Integrated Engineer: Combining Technical Ability and Leadership Prowess *by Steven T. Cerri, is an eye-opening journey for the technical person who wishes to understand key communication issues that may be hampering personal success at work. Steven T. Cerri offers a thorough analysis of the most common communication stumbling blocks experienced by engineers or scientists. His "Limiting Belief Cycles" and "Gems of Wisdom" are brilliant new ways for technologists to approach how they perceive and relate to others.*

Having worked with Steven for over twenty years, I can positively say that he is an example of a technical person who has become a master communicator. He teaches what he practices in everyday life! In The Fully Integrated Engineer: Combining Technical Ability and Leadership Prowess, *Steven offers many of the insights and tools he learned to become as confident with his "people" skills as he is with his technical expertise.*

Christine Kopec-Testolini
CEO, Avante Leadership Group

* * *

I have researched, taught and developed managers and leaders for technology driven companies for over 30 years. As a professor at the University of Washington I created a technology entrepreneurship program, lead The Boeing Corporation's aerospace management development program, worked with Microsoft and dozens of other highly competitive organizations, and developed curriculum, built faculty teams and taught at the M.B.A., Ph.D. and executive levels. But it was while I was serving as the Associate Dean for Technology Management and building de novo its now world-class masters and Ph.D. level programs, that I had the gift of meeting Mr. Cerri. In all my work, I have never experienced a management faulty member as effective as Mr. Cerri. If education in its broadest sense is to improve one's understanding and interactions with the world, then Steven is a highly effective educator and his "model" for leadership is a wonderful and significant contribution to the management field.

In 2003, I asked six of my best engineering students to take Mr. Cerri's class "So You Want to Be a Technology Manager." All tried to avoid the "unnecessary" course, claiming they had intensely busy schedules. All of them entered the class convinced that it would be their lowest priority and provide little if any value. In fact, each of those students came to me individually and reported halfway through the term that Steven T. Cerri's class was by far the most important class they had taken at University, period! "Why?" I asked. Because for the first time they had begun to understand themselves and in that knowledge caught a glimpse of how they could better understand others. Further, they had learned how to use that knowledge and insight to increase and improve their effectiveness – their relations with their lab improved, their achievements increased, they had more confidence in their abilities and set higher personal goals. They found others were accepting their "leadership."

I am not claiming Steven is a miracle worker. He is, however, an astute researcher of human behavior and a brilliant communicator. By having us focus our attention on developing models, and seeing the causal links between beliefs, attention, and emotional and physiological states, we can develop the tools and skills to lead highly technical and complex project, groups, and organizations. If one reads Steven's book and works to practice the wisdom, she or he will become a much more effective and powerful leader and significantly increase his/her own value within the organization.

Professor Gary S. Hansen
Former Associate Dean, College of Engineering, UC Santa Barbara

* * *

One of Steven's strengths as a management coach is his ability to help me shift my perspective to achieve win/win outcomes. Shifting perspectives is exactly what this book is all about. In my case, with the benefit of two stories from Steven's experience, I was able to frame an unexpected developmental test issue in a constructive light for my team and customer, leading to the delivery of compliant flight hardware and a very satisfied customer.

Leslie Buchanan
Program Manager at a large, high technology aerospace and commercial products company

* * *

Having been both a practicing software engineer and a project manager – as employee and as business owner – I've come to appreciate the challenge of effective management and team leadership. The skills needed to be successful in a technical management role are generally not taught in college engineering curriculums, and all too often no formal leadership development program exists in our workplaces. Phrases like "effective management" can be read as "good at human relationships when playing the role of manager." Steven's work presents an approach to understanding human relationships that is focused towards an audience of technical managers, but contains wisdom valuable in our other relationships as well. I wish I had come across Steven's work as I was transitioning into technical management many years ago!

Mark Andrews
Lead Engineer, Savvius

* * *

When I shook Steven's hand, I had no idea I was meeting one of the finest mentors I'd ever have.

Steven's advice is simple and relevant and it has fundamentally changed the way I approach my entire career. He helped me understand that flexibility combined with a passion for learning make for a valuable employee. I also learned about the stark difference between people who remain focused solely on the technical aspect of their career and those who practice positive collaboration. The invaluable wisdom Steven shared with me has given me a passion for continuous learning, the application of which has helped me join aerospace projects that inspire me to get up in the morning.

There is no doubt that what you read here will propel your career to new and exciting places, but what strikes me most about Steve's work is not the professional success that naturally follows after incorporating his advice, it's the joy you will find in yourself.

Thank you so, so much.

Uma Verma
Aeronautical Engineer

* * *

3

If You Are an Engineering or Technical Manager, Read This

If you are an engineering manager, then you know that people who select certain professions, generally, have typical ways in which they move through the world. Engineers and technologists are no exception. In general (yes, I am making a huge generalization here, but it is useful, nonetheless) engineers see the world and respond to it in specific ways, sometimes in ways that make them easy to manage and sometimes in ways that make them a challenge to manage.

You have people who report to you who are from all over the world, from a wide variety of backgrounds, with a wide variety of temperaments, and of different generations, and your job is to align those individuals into a team. And unlike the engineers who want to change their behaviors in order to advance, as the manager, your job is to influence behavior when people do not even know they need to modify their behavior. You are on the outside looking in, and while you may have positional authority, it often seems like it is too little influence in relation to what you would like.

In this book you will find tools you can use to make your management job easier. I will discuss management techniques, generally, in the next several chapters. Then, beginning with Chapter 9, I will address different, specific Limiting Beliefs, one by one, and how to remedy them. As a manager, you can use each Limiting Belief chapter as a starting point to help you manage your employees more effectively. Here is a summary of how a manager might use this book.

The Fully Integrated Engineer: Combining Technical Ability and Leadership Prowess, First Edition. Steven T. Cerri.
© 2016 The Institute of Electrical and Electronics Engineers, Inc. Published 2016 by John Wiley & Sons, Inc.

Limiting Beliefs: Each of the limiting beliefs, which exists in its corresponding Map of the World, is associated with a less-than-productive set of behaviors that you probably have observed in one or more of your technical employees but have not quite understood what to do in response.

Gem of Wisdom and Focus of Attention: Along with each Limiting Belief, there is also listed a corresponding Gem of Wisdom and Focus of Attention. I strongly encourage you to focus most heavily on the Gem of Wisdom and the associated Focus of Attention. These are the two components where you can apply the most leverage to influence behavior in your employees. Focusing on the behavior in order to change the behavior of an employee is the most ineffective way to achieve the outcome you want, contrary to what others might say. However, focusing on the Map of the World, the Gem of Wisdom, and the associated Focus of Attention will provide you with a significant influence in positively modifying the behavior of your employees.

In each case of a limiting belief, the key is to focus on the Gem of Wisdom, the Map of the World, and the Focus of Attention, and using this information, have discussions with your employee regarding these topics. This process will provide you with a much more powerful impact on workplace behavior.

4

Is Free Will Truly "Free"?

I am now going to venture into the realm that many do not dare go. The realm of this discussion is *free will*. The question I am asking is not the classic question of "Does free will exist?" Rather, the question I am asking is this:

> How much of our behavior is really a result of choice and free will, and how much of it is a result of our own deterministic, relatively inflexible, internal, neurological programming?

That is the question of this chapter and I believe it is the foundation of real and effective influence, management, and leadership.

Do You Choose What You Eat?

Do you have a favorite food? Do you have a favorite dessert perhaps? I have three desserts at the top of my list. They are, in no particular order, banana split, vanilla ice cream with chocolate fudge swirl, and warm peach cobbler *à la mode*.

It does not matter what is on the dessert menu; if one of these three items is on the list, I will pick one of these three. All other desserts are not even in contention.

The point is that when one of these three desserts is available, I ultimately, will "choose" that one. Or so it seems that I am choosing.

The Fully Integrated Engineer: Combining Technical Ability and Leadership Prowess, First Edition. Steven T. Cerri.
© 2016 The Institute of Electrical and Electronics Engineers, Inc. Published 2016 by John Wiley & Sons, Inc.

I return to my original question. Do you have a dessert or a food that when you see it, all other possibilities are no longer considered? Do you have a food that seems to be your preferred choice whenever it is available, at least 95% of the time?

If your answer is yes, the next question is, "Are you choosing that preferred food?" Most people will answer unequivocally, "Yes, I am choosing that food. I have free will and I choose that food." They will respond that when they see that food they "choose" to have it. They like it. They prefer it. They proclaim that they could just as easily choose not to have it, but I beg to differ.

A Hypothetical Situation That Is Very Real

For the sake of an example, let us assume that you have a favorite ice cream. And let us further assume that you walk into an ice cream parlor and you begin to review the different ice cream flavors available. You notice your favorite flavor at the very beginning of the ice cream display case. But you "decide" that you may be in the mood for something different today. So you tell yourself that you will first look at all the other possible flavors offered in order to ensure that you are, indeed, choosing whatever ice cream you prefer at this moment. This may be a conscious decision or it may be unconscious. You continue down to the end of the ice cream display case, and at the end you are ready, now, to make your selection. You select your favorite ice cream. Again.

The questions are these: "Was that a choice?" "Did you really choose your favorite ice cream ... again?"

I say that if you choose this ice cream 95–99% of the time, then it is not a choice. It was a programmed response. In fact, in a very real sense, you had NO choice.

Here is what I think happens in this and similar situations. What I am about to describe is a model of human behavior. This model is based on my own personal experience and my observations. Neuroscientists may consider this to be a bit too simplistic and too straightforward, but I offer it as a model of what I perceive to be happening when we think we are making a choice—the same choice—over and over and over again [1].

Step 1: **You walk into the ice cream store and see your favorite ice cream in the display case along with all the others.** In this example, you see your favorite ice cream at the beginning of this process. However, the same process and outcome would occur even if you see your favorite ice cream near the end of the display case.

Step 2: **Your logical mind decides to look at all the ice cream flavors available before making your "choice."** You think to yourself that perhaps it would be interesting to have a different ice cream this time. So you tell yourself that you will wait until you have reviewed all the ice cream offerings before making your choice.

Step 3: **Your unconscious mind begins the process of remembering the last time you had your favorite ice cream.** This is an even more powerful process than you might think due to the fact that you know what your favorite ice cream tastes like and you may have no idea what all the others might taste like. Therefore, while you are looking at all the possible choices available, your unconscious mind and your physiology are going through the following processes.

A. **Your eyes have seen your favorite ice cream and, in your mind, you imagine and remember the last time you had your favorite ice cream.** While this may be out of your conscious awareness, it can be very powerful because you may be experiencing it on various sensory levels. You may see, in your mind's eye, the last time you had your favorite ice cream. You may hear yourself ordering your favorite ice cream. You may feel yourself grasping the cup of your favorite ice cream and taking a bite of it.

B. **Your taste buds remember the taste of that ice cream** and the chemicals in your mouth actually begin to change in response to the memory of that ice cream experience. (If you doubt that this could be happening, just close your eyes and imagine a juicy piece of a lemon just a few inches from your nose. Do you begin to smell the lemon? Does your mouth begin to salivate in anticipation of tasting the lemon? This is what I suggest is happening when you consider having your favorite ice cream.)

C. **Your stomach may begin to produce the gastric juices** necessary to digest that specific ice cream.

D. **Your blood sugar and blood chemistry** may begin to alter in anticipation of your favorite ice cream.

E. **Your hormonal balance may shift** as if you had already ingested the favored ice cream [1].

F. **Your whole body may begin to gear up** in anticipation of the ice cream that is now a full memory-experience from the last time you had this ice cream.

Step 4: Finally, when you are ready to make your "choice" and order your ice cream, your whole being "has already tasted and consumed" your favorite ice cream. Therefore, making your "choice" and purchasing your favorite ice cream only makes physical what your whole being has already experienced.

If you doubt the validity of the model I have presented above, just trust your own experience. Bring forth a vivid memory of your favorite food. See it in your mind's eye. Imagine the last time you had this favorite food and how good it tasted. Now notice how you feel. What is happening in your stomach? What is happening to your tongue and mouth? Are you producing more saliva than usual? Is your neurology imagining actually having your favorite food? I would be very surprised if you are not already re-experiencing what you experienced that last time you had this delicious food. I would submit that our own experience supports my hypothesis that we have neurological programs that can "run" in our neurology absent external physical experiences. And if it can happen with food, how many other categories of behavior can be influenced in this way?

Therefore, I would say that ultimately, many times a day, when we believe that we make a choice, we do not. It is not a choice. It is the end result of, what I believe, is a neurological and physiological program that has run its course. It is the end result of a sequence of neurological, physiological, and chemical actions and reactions that are embedded in your body-mind. When they are "set off" or "triggered," in this case by the external stimulus of seeing your favorite ice cream, they run, and they run from beginning to end, unless interrupted [1].

You may think that I have created this model and this example for my own purposes, so I can explain and defend my ideas. So let me give you another example for your consideration, an example that may well connect with your own personal experience. It has to do with public speaking. Here is the model as I see it.

Many people are afraid of public speaking. If you are one of those who is fearful of standing before a crowd to speak then all I have to ask you is this: "When you are on stage standing before a group of people and perhaps your palms are sweating, your heart is racing, and your vision is blurred, how does that happen? Do you think logically "I want to have sweaty palms. I want to have a fast beating heart. I want to have blurred vision."

Of course not. Something else has occurred—something that is out of your conscious control. I would say that your neurology has run your, "I am afraid of public speaking neurological program."

Personal Behavioral Subroutines

We all have these neurological programs. I call them our Personal Behavioral Subroutines (PBSRs). PBSRs are nothing more than the neurological programs, the neurological software, that dictate how we are going to respond to certain stimuli. Some programs are stronger than others. That is, some are so strong that they run completely out of our conscious awareness and are difficult to overcome; for example, a fear of heights. If we have a fear of heights, the fear that results as we contemplate standing at some significant height can be so strong as to be difficult if not seemingly impossible to overcome.

Other personal programs can be weak. Perhaps you are afraid of heights, but you still can force yourself to approach a window on the 30th floor of a high-rise building knowing that there is a window between you and the imagined fall you could take.

I would postulate that inside our conscious brain, while it may appear that we are making conscious choices, alas, it is often an illusion. Our conscious mind makes it look like we are making a choice. But in reality, I would say that there is often no real choice. There is only a program that runs and runs and runs and runs.

I believe that most of what we do, most of our actions, are governed by these personal subroutines. If this model is an accurate representation, then it means that the behaviors that you have, that you have developed over the years of training in college, the behaviors that you think represent choices on your part, are nothing more than PBSRs that run in your life and in your head and in your body.

Now, let me be clear. I do believe that free will exists. However, free will exists primarily when we are aware that we have subroutines that run and that we must overcome these subroutines in order to actually exercise choice. Only when I know that I have a program for "fear of public speaking" can I intervene and "install" a different program or a different behavioral choice to override the baseline subroutine that has been running in the past.

Limiting Beliefs and Personal Behavioral Subroutines

Each Limiting Belief that I have identified in this book, I would suggest, is a PBSR that was most likely "installed" in your neurology during your college years and will, if not amended, interfere with your career advancement. Most of the time, these PBSRs are installed covertly. Often, you do not know they are being installed, and often your professors and others around you do not know they are participating in the installation either. But it is going on.

Obviously, your parents installed some of your subroutines, while your elementary and high school teachers installed others. Some were installed by your friends and enemies, and some by your professors and friends in college. If you truly made as many choices as you think you make, your life would be chaotic. Therefore, the goal is not to eliminate PBSRs altogether. You cannot. They are an integral part of life. You can, however, replace detrimental subroutines with useful subroutines. The subroutines that were useful in college and in your early career are often not useful in a long-term technical or management career.

In this book, I have identified **15 PBSRs** that most engineers have had installed into their neurology by the time they leave college. I call them **Limiting Beliefs**. They were useful at a certain phase of your life but they will probably be a hindrance as your career advances. I have also identified **15 Gems of Wisdom**, which are 15 alternative PBSRs that will lead you down the path of greater career success. I have incorporated them in this book in the hope that they will help you move your career forward.

Just for Managers

One more major point; for all those managers who think their employees are actually choosing to be difficult, obnoxious, or uncooperative at work, you will now be able to understand that most people who you see as behaving in an unacceptable manner are merely functioning according to personal internal subroutines.

As a manager, when you are unable to determine why an employee behaves in a self-destructive manner, you now ought to be asking yourself these questions; "What Personal Behavioral Subroutine is operating?" "What are the automatic responses that I am seeing in this person's behavior?" This type of questioning will soon take the mystery out of the behaviors of those around you and give you some alternative ways of dealing with them. Understand a person's personal subroutines and you more easily understand the person. Understand a person's subroutines and you can more effectively deal with that person.

Personal Subroutines Can Help as Well as Hinder Functionality

There are many personal subroutines that people utilize. Perhaps the number is in the hundreds or maybe even the thousands. That, however, does not pose a difficult management situation because it has been my experience that most of the time managers are only required to deal with a few subroutines that dictate an employee's behavior at work.

In fact, during my career as an engineer, manager, leader, mentor, and coach, I have found only a handful of detrimental behaviors that repeatedly show up that adversely affect career growth. They repeatedly show up because our educational system teaches this limited number of behavioral patterns to engineers, scientists, and technologists and they become perceived patterns for technical success. I have selected 15 PBSRs that tend to be seen as behavior patterns that will lead an engineer, especially a young engineer, to success.

While others may find exceptions to my list, the PBSRs I present in this book are what I consider to be the major predictable patterns that engineers develop as they acquire the skills dominant in the engineering community.

In this book, I present each PBSR initially as an impediment to a successful career. I also present the ways in which each subroutine functions and how it can be changed to function in a very different, much more positive and constructive way. In fact, the goal is to transform each initial PBSR (i.e., Limiting Belief) into a more success-oriented PBSR (i.e., Gem of Wisdom).

Turning Limiting Beliefs into Successes Using Gems of Wisdom

Let us return to the ice cream example for a moment. In order for me to truly have a choice regarding my selection of an ice cream, I first must understand that I do not normally exercise choice. I first must understand the mechanism by which I usually select my ice cream.

Once I understand the process, I can then, and only then, actually choose to override my usual approach if that is my desire. Awareness of the lack of choice is first necessary in order to move toward true choice.

That is what this book is about; turning your Limiting Beliefs into successful behaviors through the application of Gems of Wisdom. Adopting this process means being able to reject old, Limiting Belief subroutine-driven behaviors and choose, instead, Gem of Wisdom subroutine-driven behaviors that are more effective in a specific situation. From my experience, this is how real choice comes about.

Reference

[1] G. Claxton, *Intelligence in the Flesh: Why Your Mind Needs Your Body Much More Than it Thinks*, Yale University Press, New Haven and London, 2015.

5

The Way You Change

In order to start off properly, we need to address the fundamental model of human action, which includes communication. This chapter will define a model—my model—of the way in which human beings, generally, move through the world. Granted it is a model, but I believe it is a Map of the World that allows us to understand why people do the things they do. It will help you to understand why you do the things you do and how to change your behaviors, if you want to. It will also inform you as to how to more effectively influence those around you.

Engineering Is Easy. It Is the People That Are Difficult

There are several generally accepted ideas held by many, if not most people, including engineers, scientists, technologists, and technical managers. The first idea is that people are mysterious and unpredictable creatures. For the typical engineer, scientist, or technologist, this idea often takes the form of a statement such as, "Science and the laws of physics are predictable and consistent. People, on the other hand, are just about as predictable as the weather."

Second is the idea that people never tell you what they truly mean. In other words, there is always something hidden in what people say and the best we can do is guess at their true meanings and intentions.

The Fully Integrated Engineer: Combining Technical Ability and Leadership Prowess, First Edition. Steven T. Cerri.
© 2016 The Institute of Electrical and Electronics Engineers, Inc. Published 2016 by John Wiley & Sons, Inc.

And third is the idea that it is much easier to deal with the laws of physics, or software, or circuitry, or biology, or dynamics, or geology, than it is to deal with the constant emotional unpredictability of people.

I consider the above perspectives to be general misconceptions regarding human interaction. I believe very differently, and, in fact, I believe that people are very predictable, very consistent, and very honest. Here are several perceptions about human communication and interaction that I believe to be true.

People are not mysterious and unpredictable but rather are predictable and easily understood—so much so that we would all be embarrassed if we knew just how predictable we really are. (Remember my previous discussion regarding Personal Behavioral Subroutines?)

People are usually telling you exactly what they mean if you know how to notice, question, and listen for it. People are almost literal in their communication, much of the time.

Dealing with people can be just as easy and enjoyable as dealing with engineering and science and the laws of physics.

In fact, whether you are a technical manager or an engineer/individual contributor, here is a question I would like you to consider:

"What would it be like if you could be as successful dealing with people as you are dealing with your technology?"

The answer to this question lies in your ability to understand the differences in the behaviors and traits that make you a successful engineer versus those that make you a successful engineering team member, team lead, or engineering manager. The distinction is the difference between what you learned in college versus what you need to learn after college.

Humans Are Just Satellites on Earth

Some of you who work in the aerospace industry may work on satellites. As we know, satellites orbit the Earth or planets, or they roam the solar system or the universe performing tasks, taking action, and gathering data.

Some types of satellites are designed to map the solar system, or the universe, or the terrain of a planet. These satellites are designed with sensors that take in data and evaluate it to produce a specific map of the object or region under observation.

I believe people are just like these satellites. In fact, human beings are just human satellites moving through the universe gathering data about that universe. From birth we roam the world gathering information about our universe, the universe known as *our life*.

Every human being has five major observational senses and with those five senses, with those five instruments of our human bodies, we take in data and information about the universe we find ourselves in, the universe of this physical reality. (Note: While we might argue that there are more than five senses, for the sake of this example and discussion the five, generally accepted senses will do.)

From the data brought in by our eyes, ears, skin, tongue, and nose, from the data initially in the form of electrical impulses, we construct our **Map of the World,** the map of our "solar system." We construct our **Map of Reality.**

Each of us, every human being, creates a unique map of the world. It is unique because our experiences are all slightly different as is our genetic makeup. Our maps of the world also have some commonalities.

For example, we all have a common experience of the fruit we collectively agree to call *strawberry*. On the other hand, each of us, probably, has a very different experience regarding the taste of a strawberry. There really is no way to know for sure if your taste of strawberry is the same as mine, but it is a good bet that they are different. So while we all agree to call this thing a strawberry, and we all agree it tastes sweet, we cannot be certain that each of use tastes strawberry in the same way.

Therefore, on one level, we all agree that we will call "the red thing that looks like this" a strawberry. But, on another level, each of us has a unique experience of the taste of the strawberry, and presently, it is impossible to know if what you taste as a strawberry is what I taste as a strawberry. My taste of strawberry is stored in my Map of the World. Your taste of strawberry is stored in your Map of the World. Everything we each experience and imagine is stored in our respective Maps of the World.

The significant similarities and differences in our maps allow us to accomplish a great deal. The similarities allow us to live together, to have language, to have an ability to cooperate. The differences give us our unique perspectives and our unique values, motives, and behaviors.

The data we gather from the world of our experiences we integrate into some form of meaningful map of the world that guides us as we move through that world. It helps us to avoid the perceived obstacles that might be in our path as well as navigate the terrain of life to achieve our desired outcomes.

In fact, our map of the world is the first step in the model of human behavior I have created. The model consists of a sequence of four steps that drive our behaviors and interactions with the various aspects of the world we interpret through the map we create. Those four steps form a feedback loop that constantly updates our world-view and our actions in that world. It is the way we learn, adapt, adjust, act, and react. It forms the structure of who we are. It ultimately forms the way in which we lead, follow, and cooperate with others. Understanding this process is the core of understanding technical management and leadership, and understanding what you must do in order to achieve long-term success in your technical career. So let us look at the four stages we human satellites use to move through our universe of life.

The Model of Human Behavior: The Four Stages to Action

My behavioral model consists of the four stages leading to action and the four stages operate as a continuous feedback look. The four stages are as such:

First Stage: The creation/generation of a **Map of the World.**

Second Stage: The creation/generation of a **Focus of Attention** generated by the map of the world.

Third Stage: The creation/generation of **Emotional and Physiological States.**

Fourth Stage: The creation/generation of **Actions and Behaviors** generated by the previous three stages.

These four stages operate continuously, 24 hours a day, 7 days a week, 365 days a year. They are represented graphically in Figure 5.1 and collectively I call them the **Cycle of Influence**.

First Stage: Map of the World

Let us look at each stage in this cycle and determine how each stage generates a unique component of our lives.

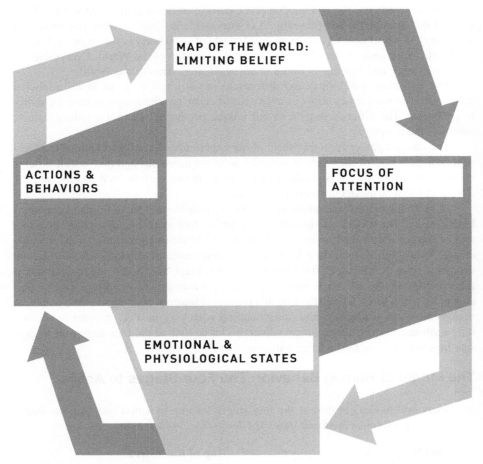

FIGURE 5.1. The Cycle of Influence. This is my general human behavioral model and represents the four stages that people move through in creating action.

The **map** of reality we generate from the electrical impulses our physical senses provide to us can be considered the first stage in our **Cycle of Influence**. (We can begin anywhere in the Cycle of Influence, but beginning at the Map of the World makes the most sense as you will see in a moment.) Our senses take in information about what we experience. It is raw electricity. Somehow, we transform those electrical impulses into a sensory experience in our bodies and our minds. Those sensory experiences take the form of what our eyes see in our world; what our ears hear as our sounds, what our skin feels as our touch; what our tongue and nose taste as our flavors, and what our nose smells as our smells.

There are large amounts of sensory input data that are disregarded or ignored in this process. The sensory input data we do accept somehow is transformed into our "construct" of our conscious reality, the way things look, sound, feel, taste, and smell. This then is our **Map of the World.**

It is personal. It is ours. You have yours and I have mine. It can be weak, such as those personal preferences you do not care much about, like whether you take out the garbage now or an hour from now. It can also be strong such as those topics you care deeply about, like whether your boss talks to you with respect or yells at you.

In 1957, the American linguist Noam Chomsky published a book in linguistics titled *Syntactic Structures*. He formulated a model of human communication including the process by which people transform their experiences into communication with others. He postulated that our experiences function as filters determining what is absorbed from new experiences. Incorporating Noam Chomsky's model of Distortion, Deletion, and Generalization into my model the next step in my Cycle of Influence model looks like this.

As new data comes into your Map of the World, it either fits your current Map or it does not. If it does fit some form of your already-existing map, it is generally labeled as recognizable information and as recognizable information it is accepted and filed away.

If the new data do not quite fit, but are close, they can be modified in some way so that it is "like" some other data you already have. It can be made to be like your already existing data by changing or modifying something. If the modification makes the new data look, sound, smell, taste and/or feel like data you already have, then it is accepted with this modification. This is known as **distortion**. *Example: "That fish I caught was 20 inches long!" (when in reality it was only 10 inches long, but it is still a fish you caught.)*

If the new data are close but do not quite fit because they contain just a few extraneous pieces of data, then those offending data may be eliminated. And if the resulting packet of data remains intact, the new, cleansed data are accepted. If none of it is acceptable then it is all rejected. This process is known as **deletion**. *Example: You go to the cupboard to find a bottle of spice. You are convinced it is not there. You return five minutes later and you now notice it. You deleted it from your focus of attention the first time you visited the cupboard.*

If the new data are close but do not quite fit, they can be absorbed into some larger data category and included in the group that already exists in your Map. The new data can be included under the classification of a general topic. This is known as **generalization**. *Example: It is absolutely impossible for anyone to cook a dish of liver* *and onions and make it taste good. It always tastes bad.* (You generally know you have a generalization when you hear or read the words, always and never. They generalize all included experiences into one, giant category.)

If the new data do not fit any previously received information, but the new data are deemed important to your success and/or survival, then the new data will be added and accepted as "learning." The learning brought about by the inclusion of this new data will be accepted and a new area of your Map will be generated and access to it will be structured, so that in the future, it can be accessed and retrieved as needed.

Finally, if the new data do not fit and cannot be either **distorted**, **deleted**, or **generalized** enough to fit, or if the new data are not capable of being accepted as learning, then the new data are outright rejected, and filed as something heard, seen, read, or experienced, but not suitable to be included in your current Map of the World as behavior-generating information.

In my model, the Cycle of Influence, all data that enters through our senses is filtered in this way. Your Map of the World is continually taking data from your senses, filtering it, updating, and starting the process all over again. In this way, your Map acts as a filter, either integrating new experiences into your existing maps, adding new learning as appropriate, modifying data to conform to your current map in some fashion, or rejecting new experiential data if it is too different from the data in your current map.

Your Map of the World not only tells you what the world is like for you, it also tells you how to navigate the world so you can be successful, in your own way. In doing this, your Map of the World tells you what is important and what is not. It tells you what to focus on and what to ignore.

This leads us to the second stage, your **Focus of Attention.**

Second Stage: Focus of Attention

The Map of the World we generate **focuses our attention** on specific aspects of the world and defocuses our attention on other aspects of the world. (Although I use the singular term Map of the World, it is important to understand that your Map of the World is composed of many "contextual maps." That is, depending upon the situation you may have different maps, leading to different ways of behaving. Therefore, while I acknowledge that we all may have many, many maps, they are all combined in this discussion into the singular concept of **The Map of the World.**)

Our Maps of the World control and direct the accessibility of new experiential data by adjusting where we put our attention in the world and what we ignore (remember the process of deletion?). It adjusts and directs our focus of attention.

How powerful is this combination of Map of the World and Focus of Attention? Just look around the world to find the answer. Humans fight wars, maintain prejudices, and guard their physical, mental, and philosophical "borders" because their maps focus their attention in a certain way. Our Maps of the World and our Focuses of Attention keep scientific paradigms in place long past their usefulness and they also bring forth new paradigms when the maps scientists adopt integrate new patterns of recognition. Sometimes our collective Maps and our Focuses unite us, such as when we think of our countries of origin, or our religious affiliations, or when we think about putting a human on the Moon. And sometimes our collective Maps and Focuses of Attention divide us, such as when people clash over territory or religion or when we compete to put a human on the Moon.

The combination of our collective Maps of the World and our Focuses of Attention creates physiological and emotional states; the emotional states that divide us by creating animosity or the emotional states that unite us by creating a common sense of purpose. In my model, the emotional and physiological states, the neurological charges, must be present for action to take place. That then, is the third stage in this process, the creation of emotional and physiological states.

Third Stage: Emotional and Physiological Charge

It is important to understand that, in this model, all action is the result of an emotional and physiological charge. No charge, no emotion, equals no action. Without an emotional and physiological charge, there can be no action and therefore, no behavior. The stronger the emotional and physiological charge, the stronger and more powerful the action will be.

If we want a new action or behavior to take the place of an old action or behavior that we no longer want, then the emotional and physiological charges associated with the new, desired action or behavior must be stronger than those of the old action or behavior it is intended to replace.

Now I know that most engineers, scientists, and technologists like to think that we make our decisions using logic. Mr. Spock of *Star Trek* is our hero, right? He exemplifies the logical processes that most engineers believe they utilize when they make decisions and take actions.

From my personal experience it seems safe to say that probably all action, indeed all thought, seems to have a corresponding physiological component. And it is this physiological component that gives rise to the *charge*, the *impetus*, for action. As I stated above, "No emotional or physiological charge means no action."

In my model, the combination of your Map of the World and the Focus of Attention it generates, combine to act like a beacon in the world. When you experience what your Map has signaled you to notice in the environment, you will have the emotional and physiological response that is connected to the content in that portion of your Map. That is why when you find yourself in a high place, and if you have a fear of heights, your emotional response is triggered by the content in your map of the world labeled "fear of heights," and the content tells you to increase your heart rate, begin sweating, narrow your vision, and generate the physiological response we call fear. In my model, this is how action is generated.

Which brings us to stage four: Action.

Fourth Stage: Actions and Behaviors

In my model, **action and behavior** are the results of this whole cycle, the Cycle of Influence. Our actions and our behaviors do not arise out of some magical process. They do not even arise from logic, or from choice, in most cases. While we may think that logic rules our actions, in most cases, I believe, it does not. In most cases, our behaviors are the result of a programmed process that once set in motion, runs to its inevitable conclusion, unless interrupted.

Understand a person's Map of the World and the Focus of Attention, and nine times out of ten, you will be able to predict that person's behavior.

Therefore, as a manager, if you want to influence and lead your team members, you must understand their Maps of the World, guide and understand their Focuses of Attention, and be aware of their physiological and emotional states.

Likewise, if (as an engineer, scientist, or technologist) you want to change your own behavior, you must understand your own Map of the World, your Focus of Attention, and the physiological and emotional states that give rise to the behaviors you want to change as well as your new Map of the World, your new Focus of Attention, and new emotional and physiological states needed to generate the better behaviors you want to adopt.

What Makes an Inspiring Speech?

Answer this question. What makes an inspiring political speech?

Some would say it is the topic. Some would say it is the charisma of the speaker. Some would say it is just the timing. Some would say it is the way the speaker looks. Some would say it is the delivery.

This is the answer as I see it: The successful speaker picks a topic and "frames" that topic so that it fits, in a familiar and comfortable way, the assumed current Maps of the World of the audience. The speaker does this to the best of his or her ability. The more accurately the speaker can frame the topic to fit the general Map of the World of the audience, the more powerfully and favorably the audience will perceive the speaker.

The speaker, via the topic and content of the speech, attempts to focus the attention of the audience in a certain direction with respect to their collective and individual Maps of the World. (This does not have to be done precisely. If the speaker can connect in some minimal fashion with the audience's Maps, the individual audience members will attempt to make the rest of the connection themselves. We want to be connected to other people as long as they do not threaten us.)

Finally, the speaker, through the emotion laid into his or her speaking process, coupled with the speaker's attempt to focus the attention of the audience in a way that elicits emotion, ultimately produces enough emotion in the audience (or so it is intended) so that when the speaker finally makes the statement providing the desired action, the audience finds it an inevitable conclusion to behave as suggested by the speaker.

As far as I can tell, this process goes on in every political election and some politicians are better at this than others. It goes on every time a leader motivates those being led to act a certain way. It goes on every time a manager motivates a team to work over the weekend. It goes on every time a manager motivates his or her employees to work late on a Friday night. It goes on every time you see a television advertisement for a product, in every newspaper and magazine ad that begins to give you an "itch" to act in accordance with the advertisement's message.

This is the way we are wired, as far as I can tell. Understand the wiring and you understand how to motivate, manage, and lead people. Understand your own wiring and you understand how to change a Limiting Belief into a motivation that leads to success. Understand your own wiring and you understand how to change something that is holding you back into something that will launch you to the next level of your career success.

Close the Loop

Finally, we close the loop. As our actions and behaviors elicit responses from the world and ourselves, we update our Map of the World, and so it goes. Our actions either provide us with what we want or they do not. If we get what we want the whole cycle is stored as a success. If we do not get what we want, the cycle may be stored as a failure, or as a partial success, or remembered but not considered useful.

This cycle of action, updating, and action, is an on-going process that defines our lives. It defines each of us. As managers we must understand this loop, this cycle, if we are to refine our ability to manage and lead others. As engineers, scientists, technologists, or technical managers, we must understand this loop in order to understand ourselves. This is the first step in becoming better engineers, better managers, better leaders, and better people.

Once again, this is only a model. However, I have found this model to be extremely beneficial in understanding and influencing myself as well as others. Consider it equivalent to Classical Newtonian Physics. We know that the world is probably ruled by something closer to Quantum Mechanics than it is by Newtonian Physics. However, Classical Newtonian physics works just fine at the macro level to get us to the Moon and Mars even though we know it is an approximation of what is really going on. Consider my model in the same way. Neuroscientists may argue with my model as being too simplistic and not completely accurate. But I have found it more than adequate to help me competently manage and lead others and manage and lead myself. That works for me!

One more point. While I have drawn the graphical representation of my model as if it is moving in a clockwise direction, I understand that it does not have to move always in that direction. The arrows, depending on the circumstances, can move in any direction. However, I believe that, most of the time, the Cycle of Influence moves in a clockwise direction and that is the way I have represented it.

A Real-World Example

Here is an example of how your Map of the World helps focus your attention, which in turn creates physiological and emotional states that generate your behaviors and actions.

A Dangerous Part of Town

Assume you are on a business trip to a town you have never visited before. Assume also that you are going to dinner at a highly rated restaurant that has been recommended to you but you also have been told that the restaurant is not in a very good part of town. (This information is now held in your Map of the World.)

You arrive at the restaurant when it is daylight. When you finish your dinner you leave the restaurant and begin walking back to your car and it is late at night.

Because you have been told this is a possibly dangerous part of town, you naturally focus your attention on all those things that reinforce your Map and beliefs about this part of town. You notice that some of the streetlights are not working. You also notice that it seems very dark, and all the stores are closed for business. You notice a darkened alley to your left. You notice some people talking over by the side of the street and they seem a little ominous. (This is a giant generalization about people, how they look, in a specific context, and what it means.)

Now, because your Map says that this is a dangerous part of town, you have focused on all those aspects that reinforce the idea that it is dangerous. You focus on those things that say, "Yes indeed, this is a dangerous part of town." Your Map of the town has focused your attention in a specific way.

Your Focus of Attention generates emotional and physiological states in you. This leads you to feel a little nervous, apprehensive, and tense. These emotions lead you to walk briskly, not talking to or looking at anyone. As you walk back to your car you hold your keys in your hand as defensive weapons in case someone appears to be a threat. You arrive at your car safely and that just reinforces your perception that this was a dangerous part of town and you knew how to navigate it safely.

It Is a Safe Part of Town

Now let us try the opposite perception. Assume the exact same situation, but this time, the only thing we will change is that you have been told that this is a safe part of town though it may not look like it. Now your Map of the World has been programmed to believe that this is a safe part of town. When you finish dinner and you are on your way back to your car, things are very different.

Now you notice all the interesting stores along the street even though they are closed. You do not even notice that some of the streetlights are not working. (You have deleted them from your perception.) You only notice the stores and the cafés. And the people across the street talking seem like they are having fun. (Once again, this is a giant generalization, but this time it generates a positive meaning.) You do not even notice that there is a dark alley to your left. (Another deletion.)

Because of your Focus of Attention, your emotional and physiological states are very different than in the previous example. Now you feel relaxed, comfortable, and even a little curious. Therefore, your actions shift. You make a mental note to come back to some of these stores tomorrow. You walk slowly, looking into the store windows. You stop to read some of the menus of the restaurants on the street. You arrive at your car safely and that only reinforces that this was a safe part of town and you knew how to navigate it safely.

This example ought to clearly illustrate that this loop, this cycle, is functioning all the time. It is the way in which we are wired. It is probably not too risky to state that this is the way we function most of the time.

Changing Behavior Requires That You Push the Right "Button"

Therefore, if you want to change your behavior or the behavior of someone else, if you want to motivate others, or yourself, the most efficient way to do that is **NOT** to focus on the behavior that you want to change.

In the first example above, if you had wanted to walk back to your car in a relaxed fashion, just telling yourself to walk back in a relaxed fashion would not have made it so.

If you want to change the way you walk back to the car, it is best to focus on your **Map of the World** and on your **Focus of Attention.** It is best to "believe" that the part of town you are in is a safe place. This belief, that the area is safe, would change your whole perception of the situation, which in turn, would change your behavior in regard to that situation. Beliefs are stored in your Map of the World. Your Map is composed of beliefs that connect experiences to outcome. Beliefs are the rules that you create that say, "**This** is true because I **believe** that **this** causes **that**." Beliefs are the core structure upon which your map of the world is built. (That is why I use the term "Limiting Beliefs." Some beliefs limit our capacity and some enhance it. The Gems of Wisdom are beliefs that enhance and expand our options.)

Attempting to behave contrary to your Map of the World, contrary to your beliefs, and your focus of attention is futile. Your actions will always be in accord with your Map of the World, your beliefs, and your Focus of Attention. And the actions of others are always in accord with their respective maps of the world, their beliefs, and their focuses of attention.

Therefore, with this logic and this model, it is clear that if you want to change the way you move through the world, or if you want to change the way someone else moves through the world, like an employee, that change will not come from focusing on the action you want changed. Likewise, your ability to change a personal behavior is not going to come first from learning new skills, such as learning how to make a budget or a schedule, unless your map of the world and focus of attention are already in alignment with those new skills, those new behaviors.

Real behavioral and motivational change is generated by modifying your map of the world (i.e., your beliefs) and in changing your focus of attention. While learning new skills may be necessary for you to know what to do and how to do it, your Map of the World, your beliefs, and your Focus of Attention must be in place if your are **going to actually do it.**

Most managers place their focus on the behaviors they want their employees to adopt and on the behaviors they want eliminated. There are plenty of books and consultants who will tell managers to *"Decide on the behavior you do not want, decide on the behavior you do want, and then convey that information clearly to the employee, then positively reinforce the behavior you want and negatively reinforce the behavior you do not want."* This approach only works if the necessary Map of the World, the associated beliefs, and Focus of Attention are already in place to support the new desired behavior. If not, then first focus on modifying the Map of the World and the Focus of Attention in order to support the new, desired behavior.

While focusing primarily on behavior seems like good advice at first glance, it is really like attempting to lead a dog by its tail. Focusing on behavior is a very inefficient way to change behavior.

Behavior is the end result of a process. Start at the beginning of the process and you will have much more leverage to change your own behavior as well as the behaviors of others.

You have probably noticed that this takes the usual concept of management change and turns it on its head. For engineers wanting to move past their Limiting Beliefs and for most managers who want to be better leaders, attaining more hard skills often is not what is needed. Telling people what to do differently and how to behave differently is not the quickest way to get results.

Rather, a change in perception often is most useful and a change in perception requires a change in your Map, the beliefs you hold to be true, and in your Focus. It is the construction of these personal Maps of the World, held together by the beliefs you hold to be true, and the Focuses of Attention that is the key to your successful transition to management and your successful long-term career as an engineer or manager.

How Difficult Is it to Loose Weight?

Here is another simple example of what I mean. How many people want to loose weight? How many people want to stop smoking? How many people want to exercise regularly? How many people want to make a lot of money? In these four categories I have probably included 90% of the people in the developed countries of the world.

Now ask yourself how many books have been written on these subjects? How much information is in the world to help people achieve success in these four categories? There has probably been enough information written about these topics to fill train cars with paper. And yet, many people still do not change their behaviors. Every new book finds plenty of people willing to start fresh. Regardless of the abundance of information, the issues remain.

Why? Because telling people **what to do** to loose weight, stop smoking, exercise regularly, and make money is not going to get them there if the rest of the Cycle of Influence is not aligned with that outcome. **What to do**, or the **action to take**, is not where the leverage point is in the process of changing behavior. Change first requires a modification of a person's respective Map of the World, a change in their belief system, and a shift in their Focus of Attention. For those people who consistently want something and yet do not achieve it, it is invariably that their Map, their beliefs, and their Focus are trained on getting something other than what they say they want. Until they change that portion of their Map and Focus of Attention that drives them to go after something other than what they say they want they will continue to not get it.

Your task then, as you read this book, is to understand not just what you want to do, but also to notice what you hold in your map of the world and what beliefs you have. I have listed the Limiting Beliefs that I have seen over and over in my experience as an engineer and manager. However, in relation to certain behaviors that I put forth in this book, you may have some Limiting Beliefs that are unique to you. Notice what they are and how they keep you from achieving what you want. Also look at where you focus your attention when you are attempting to achieve what you want and notice what a better focus of attention might be.

In this book I will take you through each Limiting Belief and provide you with a better Cycle of Influence using the Gems of Wisdom so you can avoid the Limiting Beliefs and turn your capabilities into strengths going forward.

In this book I will not pay much attention to behavior except as necessary to structure our discussion. My main focus will be on your Map of the World and the associated beliefs that are necessary for success. My secondary focus will be on the Focus of Attention that the Map and beliefs generate.

Hopefully, you will have some fun and learn a good deal about yourself and others along the way.

6

The Origin of the 15 Limiting Beliefs and the 15 Gems of Wisdom

Most technical professionals complete their education prepared to be individual contributors. This is just a fact. They are prepared initially to do their work in relative isolation, to seek the right answers to the questions and problems provided to them, and to be judged and promoted on their relative individual merit.

The beliefs, traits, skills, behaviors, knowledge, and abilities that they learn in college are indeed their strengths. They are the qualities necessary for success, **in the beginning**.

However, very soon it becomes clear that what companies or organizations want is not merely those characteristics of a good individual contributor. In addition to the skills of an individual contributor, you are soon asked to display the skills of a team member; a team leader; a good communicator; someone with good people skills; a manager; a leader; a customer service representative; and a whole host of other abilities not taught to you in college. You are asked to provide capabilities for which you were not prepared.

When these new additional skills are not available to you, your career can slow, become derailed, or even come to an end. This abrupt and potentially damaging block in your path is what I call the *Engineer's Performance Wall*©. The Engineer's Performance Wall is that seemingly mysterious career block—that obstacle that confronts you when you are being asked to do more than you thought you needed to do or were trained to do as an engineer, scientist, or technologist. You are being asked to do what college did not prepare you for, and it is a surprise.

The Fully Integrated Engineer: Combining Technical Ability and Leadership Prowess, First Edition. Steven T. Cerri.
© 2016 The Institute of Electrical and Electronics Engineers, Inc. Published 2016 by John Wiley & Sons, Inc.

This, then, is the engineer's dilemma. The skills that give you success as an early technical employee are not the skills required for a successful long-term career. The skills that brought you early success will later become skills that will block your path to additional progress.

These once-wonderful skills and traits are supported by beliefs about who you are and how you should behave, beliefs probably acquired in college. I call them **Limiting Beliefs** because they keep you from achieving your full potential as an engineer, scientist, or technologist, whether that full potential is to become a technical manager or to contribute fully as a life-long professional.

During my career as an engineer, scientist, manager, leader, entrepreneur, and trainer, I have seen a number of traits over and over again in my employees and in the people I have worked with. I have noticed these traits are independent of gender, educational institution, generation, age, and type of engineering background. They are, however, common to the engineering and technical disciplines. (Some, I am certain, are also common in other disciplines, as well.) They are displayed in people to varying degrees, depending upon their life experiences to that point in time. Not many people display all 15 Limiting Beliefs to the same degree. But nearly everyone displays a few Limiting Beliefs in a strong enough manner as to ensure that those few will hold back the person's career if nothing is done to change the limiting beliefs to beliefs that are more effective and supportive.

I have tabulated what I believe to be the 15 most common career-damaging traits and behaviors and their associated beliefs. I call the 15 beliefs, housed in the Map of the World, the **15 Limiting Beliefs**. The reason they are classified as "limiting" is that although we begin our careers thinking that they will ensure success, they often become career-limiting beliefs rather than success-oriented beliefs.

As time progresses, our careers advance, and our organizations want more from us, adhering to these early beliefs actually becomes a detriment to our continued success. They begin as 15 success beliefs and then become 15 limiting beliefs as our careers mature, creating a wall in the path of our career advancement.

If these 15 Limiting Beliefs can be modified by the application of what I call the corresponding 15 Gems of Wisdom, they can generate behaviors, that will ensure a successful long-term career. Modifying the Limiting Beliefs means that they must be morphed into beliefs that allow you much more behavioral flexibility.

I have seen these 15 Limiting Beliefs produce behaviors that stifle career success. And I have seen what happens when they are modified in a very specific way, by the application of the Gems of Wisdom, to generate behaviors that lead to long-term career success.

Therefore, what you will find in this book you will not find any place else. It comes from my personal experience. It worked for me and for my employees and team members. It worked very, very well. My bet is that it can work for you, too.

7

How To Use This Book and the Structure of Chapters 9 Through 23

In order to explain the way I have laid out the chapters in this book, I will use Limiting Belief #1 as the example. This chapter presents the format for Chapters 9 through 23.

Example: Chapter 9

Career-Limiting Belief #1

Each chapter begins with a statement of 1 of the 15 career-limiting **behaviors** generated by the limiting belief discussed in the chapter. In this case one of the limiting behaviors generated by Limiting Belief #1 is: *"My ideas are my identity. Therefore, I must fight for my ideas."*

If Career-Limiting Belief #1 is Part of Your Map of the World...

Statement of Limiting Belief #1

In this paragraph you will be presented with a brief explanation and interpretation of the Limiting Belief and how it shows up in your Map of the World.

Career-Limiting Belief #1 Produces an Ineffective Focus of Attention

Example of a Focus of Attention

Every Map of the World generates a specific range of focuses of attention. In this section you will be presented with several possible focuses of attention generated by this limiting belief.

These Focuses of Attention Produce Negative Physiological and Emotional States

Example of emotional and physiological states

Each limiting belief, through its corresponding focuses of attention, generates corresponding emotional and physiological states. In this section, a list of several of the possible emotional and physiological states generated is presented. There could be others. This section presents several examples of the possible states that can generate and drive drive career-limiting behaviors.

They Generate Career-Limiting Actions and Behaviors

Example of career-limiting actions and behaviors

Finally, in this section, I present several of the possible career-limiting actions and behaviors that can be expected as the end result of the Cycle of Influence generated by the limiting belief.

Real World Example

It is important to understand how each limiting belief manifests itself. Therefore, in this section I present a real-world example of how this limiting belief might appear in a work environment. You will see and read about a real example of the actions and behaviors people display who have this Limiting Belief and I will unpack and explain the focus of attention and the emotional and physiological states that lead to the career-limiting behaviors being analyzed so you will understand the mechanics of the complete process.

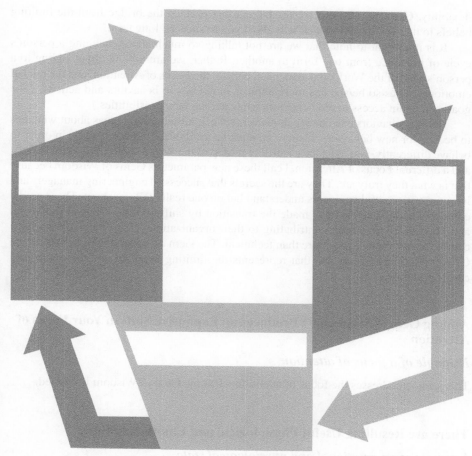

FIGURE 7.1. Career-Limiting Belief #1 and its Cycle of Influence.

This complete Cycle of Influence process is presented graphically as a figure similar to the one shown in Figure 7.1.

Add Gem of Wisdom #1 to Your Current Map of the World

Statement of the Gem of Wisdom

The Gem of Wisdom is the mental shift, the adoption of a new belief that, when applied to the Map of the World, changes the limiting belief into career enhancing behavioral flexibility. Gems of Wisdom are the beliefs that provide the bridge from the limiting beliefs to the new behaviors that will allow you to succeed long term.

It is important to note that we are not talking so much about changing a person's cycle of influence from one form to another. Rather, we are talking about adding to a person's Map of the World, the associated beliefs, the Focus of Attention, and the related emotional states so he/she has more choices in regards to behaviors and actions. (The goal is to retain access to old behaviors while adding new possibilities.)

Before behaviors can change, however, beliefs, attitudes, and ideas about what has to be true for new behaviors to show up must be available. To put it plainly, in order to behave differently, you must have a different Map of the World, a different set of beliefs, and a different Focus of Attention. I call these new parameters Gems of Wisdom because that is what they truly are. They are the secrets that successful engineering managers and long-term successful engineers understand but no one really tells us about. These model engineers and managers have made the transition by shifting their Maps of the World and Focuses of Attention, contributing to their organizations. They have made what I call the transition to being more than technical. The Gem of Wisdom will transform the Cycle of Influence from one that represents the limiting belief to one that represents career possibility.

Adding Gem of Wisdom #1 Produces an Expansive Shift in Your Focus of Attention

Example of a focus of attention

This section addresses the focus of attention when the Gem of Wisdom is applied.

There are Resulting Useful Physiological and Emotional States

Example of an emotional and physiological state

In this section I will list the emotional and physiological states generated when the Gem of Wisdom is applied.

Using Gem #1 will Generate Career-Enhancing Actions and Behaviors

Example of a career-enhancing behavior

In this section I list the actions and behaviors that, in my experience, are most likely to be displayed when the Gem of Wisdom is incorporated into the Map of the World.

Real World Example

In this section I include an in-depth example of the behaviors that result from the application of the Gem of Wisdom. This is an update of the previous real-world case

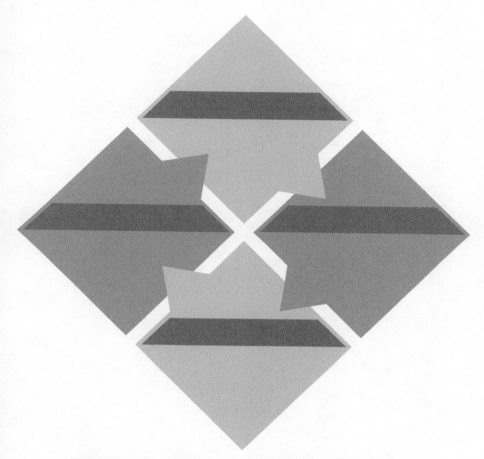

FIGURE 7.2. Gem of Wisdom #1 Alters Your Cycle of Influence.

presented at the beginning of the chapter so that you can see and understand how the Gem of Wisdom can change the behavioral outcome.

This complete process is presented graphically as a figure similar to the one presented as Figure 7.2.

Note: If you decide that you have one or more career-limiting beliefs as I present in chapters 9 through 23 and you would like to add the appropriate Gem of Wisdom, you can find a step-by-step guide on how to accomplish this addition in Chapter 8.

8

How to Add Any Gem of Wisdom to Your Map of the World

Remember, the goal is not to remove your limiting belief. There may well be times when your limiting belief and the associated behaviors are just what the situation calls for. So do not think you are wrong or need to throw away your limiting belief and behaviors. Your goal is to add choices. So the question becomes how do you add Gems of Wisdom to your current Map of the World and thereby add behavioral flexibility?

Steps to Add a Gem of Wisdom to Your Current Map of the World

Step 1: Make several copies of empty Cycle of Influence charts (see Figures 8.1 and 8.2). Make 10 or so copies. Leave only the titles of each box.

Step 2: Start with the behavior you want to change (the behavior you do not want). Write it in the Actions and Behaviors box.

Step 3: Now determine what the belief is that leads you to that behavior. In other words, what is the belief that makes this behavior acceptable in this situation or this context? This may take some new thinking on your part. Once you are clear about what the belief is that truly generates that behavior, label it your Limiting Belief and place it in the box marked Limiting Belief.

Step 4: Now ask yourself how this Limiting Belief is supported. Are there other beliefs that are connected to it? What other things do you say about this

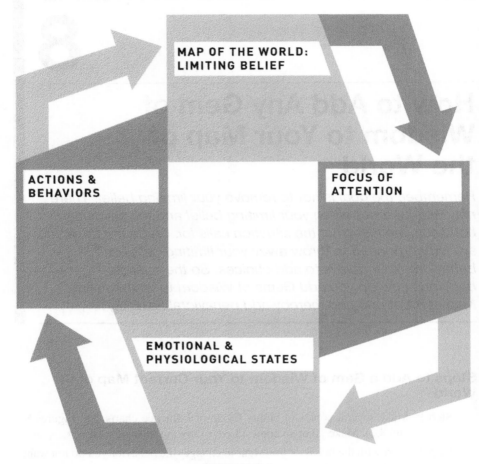

FIGURE 8.1.

limiting belief that maintains it in place; that makes it true for you? Ask yourself what you believe to be true when this limiting belief comes up for you. Be very clear how this limiting belief is phrased in your mind and how it is connected to other secondary beliefs that make it even more true and powerful.

Step 5: Next, ask yourself where you put your attention and what you notice when you hold the belief or beliefs you uncovered in Step 4.

Step 6: Next, notice what emotional state you are in when you think about your belief and you put your attention where it naturally goes when you think of your limiting belief. (This is an important step. You must "experience" the full emersion into the experience of this belief. Do the best you can to fully experience what happens to you and to your physiology when this belief is triggered along with the secondary beliefs associated with it.)

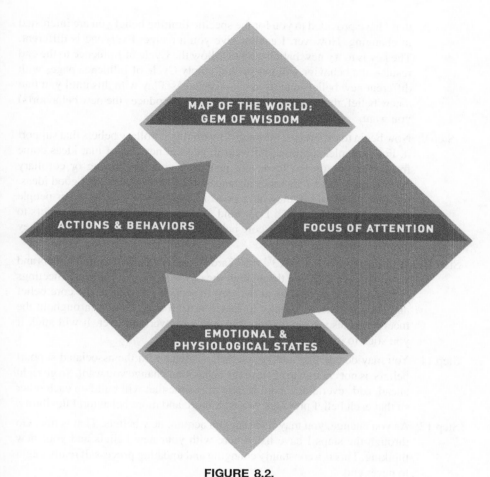

FIGURE 8.2.

Step 7: Notice how this emotional state produces an undesirable behavior pattern, a behavior pattern that you do not want as your default pattern. Check to verify that the Limiting Belief actually produces the behaviors you want to change. If not adjust the belief or your Focus of Attention. Keep cycling through the Cycle of Influence until you have a coherent experience from limiting belief to undesirable behavior.

Step 8: After you have completed Step 7 and you have a clear understanding and experience of how this cycle is generated by the Limiting Belief you hold, begin to experiment with new beliefs. Select new beliefs that undercut and refute the limiting belief or beliefs. When you do this, notice what you focus on, what you emotionally and physiological experience, and what behaviors seem to be most available to you with the new belief or beliefs. This will take some experimenting. You can start with the Gem of Wisdom that I have provided to you for the specific limiting belief you are interested in changing. However, I cannot give you a recipe. Everyone is different. The key is to try new beliefs and to follow the Cycle of Influence to the end result—the behavior. Fill out several empty Cycle of Influence pages with different new beliefs and its associated stages. Play with this until you find a new belief, that you believe to be true, that produces the new behavior(s) you want.

Step 9:   Now begin to expand the new belief by finding corollary beliefs that support it. For example, suppose you want to add the new belief that ideas come from everyone on the team, not just from you. Supporting or corollary beliefs might be: I remember instances when other people had good ideas; or other people think they have good ideas just like I do; or other people want to be heard just like I do. Find as many useful, supportive beliefs to add credibility to your new core belief and link them by thinking how they all make sense.

Step 10: Write the core belief on a 3″ × 5″ card along with the supporting beliefs and carry the card with you throughout the day at work. As you enter meetings or begin discussions look at the card to remind yourself of the core belief and the corollaries. Attempt to function from that position throughout the meeting or discussion and do this over and over and over. It will stick if you stick to it.

Step 11: You may decide that adding one belief, along with the associated support beliefs, is not enough to achieve the behavioral change you want. So go right ahead, add several new core beliefs over time that will build on each other so that each belief provides you with more and more behavioral flexibility.

Step 12: As you change, you may find that you acquire new beliefs. That is fine. Go through the steps I have listed here with your new beliefs and your new thinking. This is a constantly changing and updating process. It really ought to never end.

Step 13: Remember, your goal is not to remove your limiting belief. There may be times when it will be the appropriate course of action. You goal is to add more capability to what you already have.

Step 14: The results you achieve will probably be gradual, although in some cases, change can happen rapidly. Remember you are undoing years of neuro-logical conditioning. You will know that your new beliefs are working when you can actually choose how you want to respond instead of having a "knee-jerk" reaction. When you can actually take a breath and respond to a situation in a new way that opens up new possibilities for behavior, take a moment to congratulate yourself. You are on the path to becoming a powerful and effective member of your team.

9

Ideas as Identity:
Career-Limiting Belief #1

"My ideas are my identify. Therefore, I must fight for my ideas."

Most engineers and technical professionals personally identify with their ideas to such a degree that they believe they must fight for and defend those ideas. They see any criticism of their ideas as a personal attack. They are defensive rather than responsive to the ideas of others. As well, they do not ask others for suggestions. In order to advance in your organization and in your career, it is necessary to decouple your identity from your ideas.

If Career-Limiting Belief #1 Is Part of
Your Map of the World...

As an engineer or technical professional, throughout your college education, your answers to professors' questions were a direct reflection on you and your creativity. In fact, demonstrated creativity is often the measure of excellence in science and engineering. The answers and ideas you generated were a direct reflection of your technical prowess. It was just that simple. Excellence was reflected in your grades. Your grades

The Fully Integrated Engineer: Combining Technical Ability and Leadership Prowess, First Edition. Steven T. Cerri.
© 2016 The Institute of Electrical and Electronics Engineers, Inc. Published 2016 by John Wiley & Sons, Inc.

reflected on you. Therefore, it did not take long for your identity and your self worth to be linked to your ideas.

It is completely expected, then, that when you joined a company or organization and began to function as a professional in a team, you merely continued that college-bound behavior where good ideas meant praise. It makes perfect sense that you would defend your ideas as though they were a direct reflection of how smart and valuable you are to the company or organization. On the job, such thinking drives you to assume that anything less must mean that you are not as good as your colleagues, that you are not worthy of that big pay raise or that big bonus, or that you do not deserve a positive annual performance review. Therefore, you work under the assumption that your manager must always perceive you as the fount of brilliant ideas.

The reality is this: a company or organization cannot survive if everyone on the team functions in this way. There cannot be success if everyone fights for his or her ideas as if personal identity depends on those ideas. If all engineers display this behavior, then everyone is constantly defending individual ideas and the team cannot come to an effective integrated solution that merges the best from everyone's ideas.

Career-Limiting Belief #1 Produces an Ineffective Focus of Attention

"Who is attacking me? And why?"

When you believe that your ideas and identity are linked, your focus of attention is on those environmental data that support that position. (Remember the example of the restaurant in Chapter 5?) To support your beliefs, you look for behaviors from colleagues and signals in the environment that convince you that your ideas are being questioned; doing so leads you to the conclusion that you are being personally attacked. Your misguided Focus of Attention leads you to these kinds of stances:

- Who is attacking me?
- Do I appear competent?
- How much appreciation am I getting for my ideas?
- Does anyone have better ideas than mine?
- What will my boss think about my idea compared to the ideas of others?
- I don't want to look stupid in front of my boss or the team.
- How do I defend my ideas?

These are some of the questions and statements that describe where you may be focusing your attention when you have the belief that your identity is tied to your ideas. This Focus of Attention also generates some negative emotional and physiological states.

This Focus Produces Negative Physiological and Emotional States

The Focus of Attention generated by the notion of "ideas are identity" will often produce certain and specific negative emotional and physiological responses in many people. Some of the expected negative states generated are listed here:

- Defensiveness
- Concern about reputation
- Aggressiveness
- Stubbornness
- Fear
- Argumentativeness

These emotional and physiological states tend to generate behaviors that are not productive for teamwork.

They Generate Career-Limiting Actions and Behaviors

"I need to fight for my ideas."

Ultimately, holding onto the belief that ideas are identity produces ineffective patterns all around you. Some of the unproductive actions you may develop as a result of the Career-Limiting Belief #1 might be these:

- You will lack flexibility.
- You will be unreasonable.
- You will be argumentative.
- You will fight to defend your ideas, even when the defense of the ideas seems unreasonable and out of proportion.
- You will not acknowledge the significance or value of the ideas of others.
- You will not ask for nor take input from others regarding your ideas.
- You seem to treat ideas as competitive points to be gathered in your favor.

Real World Example: What Happens When Ideas = Identity

Tom is an engineer. He is attending a design meeting and he has been asked to present his idea for the solution to a technical problem regarding a satellite instrument for which he is responsible. He has been thinking about it for a while and is confident about his approach to the problem. At the meeting, another engineer responds that Tom's idea will not work because the power system is insufficient to supply the total electrical power requested by Tom's instrument and all the other instruments on board. Tom responds that it is the only way his instrument will work and that some other instruments will have to reduce their

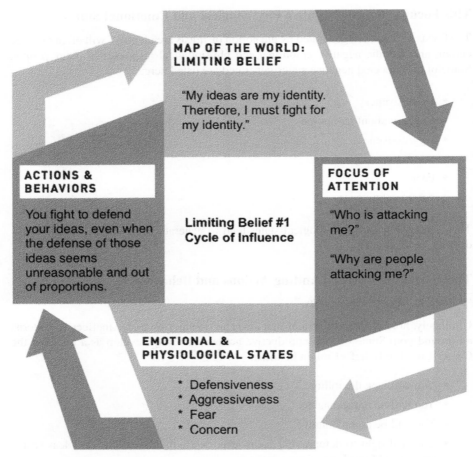

FIGURE 9.1. Career-Limiting Belief #1 and its Cycle of Influence.

power consumption. Tom is convinced his approach is the only viable solution to the problem. He makes it clear that he has given his solution a good deal of consideration, and he is convinced that his is the only possible solution. End of discussion!

Next, someone else adds that there might be another way to deal with the power consumption required by Tom's instrument. It is clear that Tom's power requirements are being questioned. Tom becomes adamant about his solution. He will not budge on this issue. He quotes the data from his analysis. He says that he is certain of the power requirements of his instrument, and he is convinced that other instruments in the system are using too much power.

The meeting seems to come to a stalemate. Tom has backed everyone at the meeting into a figurative corner, including himself, and it seems that no equitable solution can be found. It is clear that Tom is not in any mood to negotiate. Tom thinks that it would be embarrassing to reconsider his stance. The meeting leader is convinced that the situation is too fragile and potentially embarrassing and so decides this topic ought to be postponed for now.

The meeting has stalled. There is too much conflict. Lines have been drawn and so the meeting leader tables Tom's discussion and moves on to another topic. Most of the people in the room are well aware of what has happened. Tom took a very hard stance and could not back down without significantly embarrassing himself. The participants will not forget this meeting. This is the first step for Tom on the path to developing a reputation as a difficult person to work with (see Figure 9.1).

Add Gem of Wisdom #1 to Your Current Map of the World

"Good ideas can come from anywhere. Successful career growth and organizational success require the integration of different ideas."

There are obviously many different new beliefs or perceived truths that you can add to your Map of the World to turn Career-Limiting Belief #1 around. I call these new and better ways of thinking about and looking at the world *Gems of Wisdom*.

To the problem of ideas as identity, I offer this Gem of Wisdom: Successful technical managers and engineers who can fully contribute to their organizations understand that ideas can come from anywhere: from the team, the organization, even from customers and competitors. It is, therefore, important to be open to observing, integrating, and accepting ideas from a wide variety of sources, not just from yourself. Your job is not always to have the best idea but to contribute what you can and to coordinate the ideas of everyone to develop the best from them all. Also, if you are a manager and you constantly attempt to present your own ideas as the best, you will be competing with your own team members, which is an ineffective way to manage others.

While some organizations (especially some in Silicon Valley that I have observed and worked with) like to utilize an internal competitive process in an effort to ferret out the best ideas, this combative process seldom yields answers that are any better than other good, solid, forms of discussion. True leaders ultimately learn how to integrate diverse ideas regardless of their source and regardless of the level of debate utilized.

To be successful in your technical organization, in the long run, you must unlearn what made you successful in college and what made you successful as an entry-level engineer or scientist. You must be willing to merge your ideas with the ideas of others, and through this merger, develop ideas that work for the team. This is truly what it means to be part of a team: to contribute your best ideas and then work with the ideas put forth in an effort to develop the strongest idea for the team's success. And if you choose to become a technical manager, it will be your job to facilitate the merger of the best ideas, no matter their source.

Adding Gem #1 Produces an Expansive Shift in Your Focus of Attention

"Who also has good ideas?"

By looking at all possible good ideas, your Focus of Attention will shift significantly. You will find yourself asking questions like these:

- Who has ideas?
- Are these good ideas?
- Are there pieces of the ideas of others that can be put together to produce better ideas?
- What can I do to facilitate the creation and integration of various ideas?
- Who needs encouragement to put forth their ideas?
- How can I contribute to the safety of this discussion so people will put forth their ideas?

The best idea(s) will become self-evident to the group.

There are Resulting Useful Physiological and Emotional States

Your altered Focus of Attention will, in turn, generate new and more useful emotional and physiological states. Some of those more productive states are listed below:

- Curiosity and openness
- Cooperation
- Excitement
- Helpfulness
- Confidence

Using Gem #1 will Generate Career-Enhancing Actions and Behaviors

"I'll ask questions before I take a position."

By adding this Gem of Wisdom, you will shift your negative generated behaviors. In fact, below are three possible new behaviors that might result from this simple change:

1. **You will learn to ask questions, facilitating the creation and integration of ideas.**
2. **You will learn to control your emotions so you can help others feel comfortable presenting their ideas.**
3. **You will acknowledge and give credit for good ideas regardless of the source.**

Let's take a look at each of these actions and behaviors in more detail.

1. **You will learn to ask questions, facilitating the creation and integration of ideas.** A good team member or technical leader uses the art and process of asking questions in a way that determines the overlap and/or usefulness of various ideas. This process will allow ideas to form a common ground and to develop the synergy that will facilitate the emergence of the best ideas. This ability allows the differences to be analyzed and discussed openly, and, ultimately, to be integrated into a better idea that stands as a combination of all the best parts of each individual idea.

   The best way to ask these types of questions is not to have a specific agenda, but to embark on an exploration. Have a desire to explore the various ideas to see where they may provide some utility to the desired outcome of the discussion. It will be a messy process at times, but this is a creative endeavor, not a mathematical calculation. Be curious and explore the ideas to determine what fits and what makes sense.

2. **You will learn to control your emotions so you can help others feel comfortable presenting their ideas.** You need to stop fighting for your own ideas; instead, work to motivate people to provide their own ideas for discussion, analysis, scrutiny, and integration.

   Throughout my career, I have observed that people think they make decisions based on logic and reason. However, when questioned further, the core motivating force has always seemed to be emotional. That is, we often seem to be driven to act based on an emotional force and then we defend the action by forming a logical rationale to defend that action. I have seen emotion, cast as logic, sway the minds of many people.

   Therefore, my experience is that, generally, we seem to be driven to act by our emotions, not by our logic. Logic comes to the rescue in an attempt to explain why we do what we do, but it is only after the fact. It is only after the emotions have driven us to act or to prepare to act that logic comes to the fore.

   In order to provide an environment where colleagues feel comfortable having their ideas scrutinized, you must be able to control your own emotional state so you can help others feel comfortable. It is all about communicating from an emotionally stable position. Starting there, you can help the team achieve the most effective solution from all the ideas presented.

3. **You will acknowledge and give credit to good ideas regardless of their source.** A powerful behavior that results from the implementation of this Gem of Wisdom is a willingness to give credit to others. Once others see your changed behaviors, you will open the door to creativity and participation that will generate a flood of new ideas. This is what you want to achieve.

Real World Example: Gem of Wisdom #1 in Action

We look again to the previous real-world case. Tom is an engineer. He is attending a design meeting and he has been asked to present his idea for the solution to a technical

FIGURE 9.2. Gem of Wisdom #1 Alters Your Cycle of Influence.

problem regarding a satellite instrument for which he is responsible. He has been thinking about it for a while and when he presents his idea to the meeting attendees another engineer responds that his idea will not work because the system electrical power supply is insufficient. Tom, seeing a moment to gather information from his peer experts, responds by asking how much power is available for his function and how much power each of the other instrument subsystems requires.

The answer makes it clear that the allocation of power has to change but there is no use discussing it now because others have not had time to prepare for this new topic. Tom responds by saying, "Well, I have been giving this a lot of thought. If the original power I required is not available, I think I might be able to make some adjustments, but I do not think my system can function at the power level that you say is available. So, it seems to me that we will have to work together to allocate power so that all the instruments can function, probably at a lower power level than currently assigned, including mine. That will probably take some negotiations regarding power. So, I would like to ask for a side meeting in the next day or so when we can all come prepared to discuss minimum power requirements and determine what has to be done for all of the onboard instruments to get the power they require."

Notice how Tom produces a clear way to move forward. He has decoupled his identity from his idea and now the team can solve this issue together.

Note: This is not a hypothetical situation. My team members and I consistently used this processes to develop answers that produced positive results to challenging dilemmas (see Figure 9.2).

10

Being Right: Career-Limiting Belief #2

"I'm supposed to be right."

Many engineers, scientists, technologists, and technical managers want to be right. Being right as often as they can is what they were trained to do in school. They often fight to be right about something at the expense of being effective in achieving a strategic goal or tactical outcome. As you progress in your organization, you will find that the organization will reward you more often for being effective than for being right.

If Career-Limiting Belief #2 Is Part of Your Map of the World...

The first Limiting Belief, "Idea as identity," has a corollary here. The identity process ultimately becomes a battle to be right about your ideas, your position, about everything having to do with you.

Once again, being right is what we were taught in college. It might also be what your organization praises you for in the early portion of your work career. Therefore, you fight for your ideas because they are reflection of you (Limiting Belief #1), and you also fight for your ideas because you want to be right. No one gets a raise or a promotion for being wrong.

However, once you are inside an organization and you are part of a team, what is most important is not necessarily being right all the time or even getting your individual job done in a specific way. Rather, the goal is getting the team's job done. Being effective is therefore defined as being able to complete your work well while simultaneously advancing the work and goals of the team. Being effective is about everyone on the team contributing his or her best efforts, regardless of who gets the credit, so that the team can be successful. Let me repeat that last part: *Being effective means contributing to the success of the team.*

And therefore, my definition of getting the team's job done is *being effective.* Once you are in an organization, it is often less important for you always to deliver your right answer than it is for you to *contribute to the process of delivering* the right answers.

To be sure, there will certainly be times, either as an engineer or a technical manager, when staunchly taking a position and defending it is a worthwhile way of behaving. This is sometimes the only way to get a new idea into an organization. But these situations are relatively rare.

If you decide to remain a technical specialist and achieve "senior engineer" status, then being right will be a more accepted way of moving through the world. You will be perceived as an advisor, and advisors are supposed to be right. However, if you decide not to remain a specialist, and not to become a subject matter expert (SME), or you decide to become a manager, then attempting to be right much of the time will only give you a reputation for being arrogant and power-hungry.

Think of it this way. Being right worked in college. Your tests required that you provide the right answer. In your organization, however, this approach will work only under very specific circumstances. If you are an SME or if you are the most knowledge-able manager in the organization, being right can work. Otherwise, *being effective is a much more useful behavior for your long-term career success.*

Career-Limiting Belief #2 Produces an Ineffective Focus of Attention

"I must stand my ground."

When you are thinking that is it better to be right than to be effective, you will often expend your energy standing your ground to prove your ideas are better than the ideas of others. Some of the questions or perspectives on which you might focus your attention are listed below:

- They must be wrong. I will show them how.
- What's wrong with the ideas of others? Where can I find weakness in their work?

- I'll make sure I convince others that I'm right in the meeting and then check my data later.
- I don't want to give a wrong answer in front of my manager or colleagues.

This Focus Results in Negative Physiological and Emotional States

Those Focus of Attention questions and statements will produce certain specific emotional and physiological responses, most of them based in some kind of fear that your work will be found wanting. You may experience the following states:

- Defensiveness
- Fear
- Illusiveness
- Lack of openness
- Aggression

Fearful States Generate Career-Limiting Actions and Behaviors

"I will find a way to make the ideas of others seem wrong and my ideas seem right."

Ultimately, your Map of the World and your Focus of Attention generate potentially damaging emotional and physiological states that generate the impetus for career damaging action. Some of the actions that clearly represent Limiting Belief #2 are these:

- You will defend your ideas seemingly to unreasonable ends.
- You will not listen to the ideas of others.
- You will raise your voice or go silent and become passive.
- You withhold information from others.
- You will focus on an issue to the exclusion of other, equally important, issues.
- You will even disagree when someone brings up a response that is aligned with a position you previously supported.

Real World Example: Your Need to be Right = Negative Outcomes

Barbara is in a discussion with three other software engineers. They are working on a large software program and each is responsible for a specific section of the program. Barbara has implemented a complex algorithm; Judy, one of the other programmers, is convinced that Barbara's implementation takes too much time to run and has told her so. Since this is a real-time program, processing time is critical. Barbara is convinced her implementation of the algorithm is most efficient. She will not listen to anyone else's ideas regarding the implementation of her algorithm. No matter what Judy says, Barbara's response is consistently, "My implementation is the most efficient possible.

There's no way to speed it up." Barbara is convinced she is right and she is convinced that she must defend her position.

Barbara's Map of the World contains a series of Limiting Beliefs having to do with the general idea that, if she is a good programmer, she must know how to implement this algorithm as efficiently as possible herself.

Her Focus of Attention is on ensuring that she does not appear to need the help of others to do her job. And her emotional and physiological states include defensiveness and aggression. Predictably, she defends her coding and algorithm implementation and rejects any contributions from others.

A graphical representation of the Career-Limiting Belief #2 Cycle is presented in Figure 10.1.

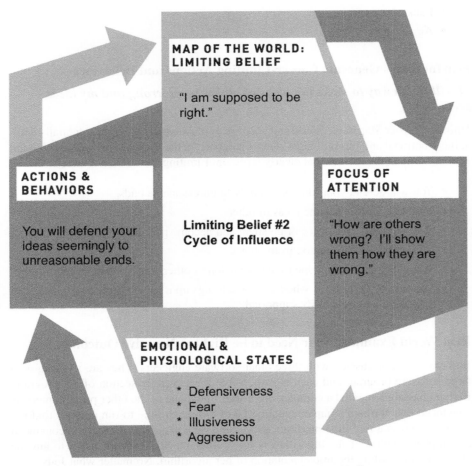

FIGURE 10.1. Career-Limiting Belief #2 Cycle of Influence.

Add Gem of Wisdom #2 to Your Current Map of the World

"I understand that being right is giving credit to myself. Being effective is giving credit to others, as well. My long-term career success is dependent upon being effective. I recognize the strengths of others. Therefore, I can support their best talents more often."

The first step in exploding Limiting Belief #2 is to understand that while new employees or new individual contributors are paid to be right, technical managers, successful career engineers, and their successful team members and colleagues, are paid to be *effective*. No company or organization will look favorably upon a situation in which either the individual contributor or manager was right but the project ultimately failed. The organization's management only wants a successful outcome to be achieved. *Being effective is a better metric to achieving success than being right.*

Adding Gem #2 Produces an Expansive Shift in Your Focus of Attention
"Where is each person right about something?"

Adding the above secret to your map will shift your Focus of Attention to finding the best in all of the ideas that contribute to the solution. Enacting curiosity can tap into the best from everyone. You may find yourself asking questions like these:

- Where is each person right about something?
- How do I keep the team or group focused on moving forward, not on giving criticism?
- What is the best part of each idea presented?
- How do I get out of the way of the team succeeding?
- How do I contribute to the team's success?

There are Resulting Useful Physiological and Emotional States

The shift of focus toward curiosity will, in turn, generate new and positive emotional and physiological states. Some of the positive states you might experience are:

- Curiosity
- Excitement
- Calmness
- A willingness to question

Using Gem #2 will Generate Positive Actions and Behaviors

"I will compliment people for the good work they have done."

By adding the Gem of Wisdom #2 to your Map of the World, you will invariably generate new behaviors that will show your wisdom in relying on the collective knowledge of the entire team. See Figure 10.2.

1. **You will compliment people for the good work they have done.**
2. **You will ask questions of others in order to discover their ideas.**
3. **You will work to combine the best parts of different ideas from everyone to create an environment that fosters collaboration.**

Let's look at each of these actions and behaviors in more detail to determine how they might shed light on more general behaviors that may develop from this Gem of Wisdom.

1. **You will compliment people for the good work they have done.** Just as you must understand your own strengths and weaknesses in order to achieve career success, it is important to be able to recognize, understand, and especially deal with the strengths and weaknesses of others. Most of us can often notice the strengths and weaknesses of others, but the gem here is to have this understanding in such a way that you can more often support the best talents of others in spite of their weaknesses. You do not want to make anyone feel wrong or inadequate (yourself included).

    The secret is in supporting the best in others while minimizing their weaknesses. Being able to focus on the positive and diffuse and divert attention away from the negative dissipates any desire to be right. To paraphrase Peter Drucker, the secret is to amplify the strengths of people and make their weaknesses irrelevant. In this way, seeing others as attacking you or seeing them as aggressors is minimized. This shift of focus from you to the success of others is critical in exploding Limiting Belief #2.

2. **You will ask questions of others in order to discover their ideas.** Often, we assume that others will tell us what is important and essential. However, some people have the belief that being proactive in managing or contributing to a discussion is intrusive and arrogant. But, finding a gracious way to get key information from the SMEs is an incredibly useful talent.

    Remember, people are often unsure of what their place is in a discussion. They are nervous to contribute because they do not want to be off-base. As a manager, your understanding and respect will provide a comfortable way to engage. Being curious shows that you can be a proactive agent, assisting others in communicating their ideas openly. You can become a catalyst for discussion and idea generation.

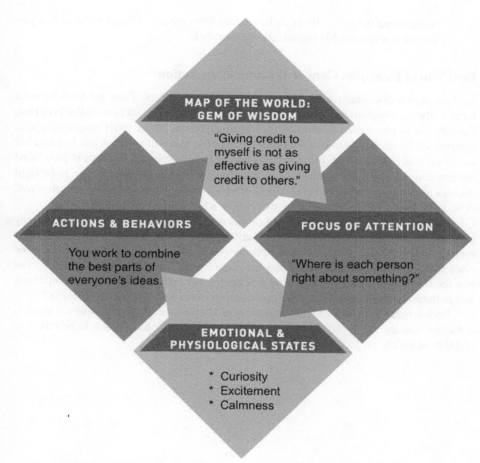

FIGURE 10.2. Career Enhancing Gem of Wisdom #2 Cycle of Influence.

3. **You will work to combine the best parts of different ideas from others to create an environment that fosters collaboration.** Few people are gifted with the ability to develop a successful idea from beginning to end without the input from others. Ideas become better with the addition of modifications from others. In fact, most great ideas, most technical and scientific solutions, are the result of a great deal of give-and-take discussion. Why would we be willing to accept that great ideas need this to-and-fro process, but not smaller ideas?

Indeed, your behavior resulting from this gem is to initiate and foster the to-and-fro discussion that allows ideas to be analyzed and dissected in order to extract the best from each. Then each of these bits of ideas that are so powerful can be combined and integrated to create ideas and solutions that are more powerful than any one standing alone. This is the art of facilitation. Being able to facilitate the generation of a better idea from pieces of lesser ideas makes you an extremely valuable organizational member.

Real World Example: Gem of Wisdom #2 in Action

Barbara is in a discussion with three other software engineers. They are working on a large software program and each is responsible for a specific section of the program. Barbara has implemented a complex algorithm; Judy, one of the other programmers, is convinced that Barbara's implementation requires too much time to run and has told her so. Since this is a real-time program, processing time is critical. Barbara is convinced her implementation of the algorithm is most efficient but rather than fighting to be right decides to ask Judy for more information. Barbara responds to Judy with the question, "Ok, Judy, how would you speed up my code or what would you do differently?"

Since processing time is so critical in this application, Barbara would not win any points by being obstinate. It would serve Barbara better to *be effective,* which means that either it will be shown that her code is optimum and Judy is wrong, or Judy (or someone else) will speed up Barbara's code and the program will be improved. It just does not pay for Barbara to fight to be right and risk having her code be a processing bottleneck and perhaps be proven wrong farther downstream in the implementation process.

Barbara and Judy work together to analyze Barbara's code to determine if there is a way to increase the speed. The bottom line is that Barbara has chosen to be effective and it benefits the project, the team, and ultimately, Barbara.

11

What versus How: Career-Limiting Belief #3

"What I say is much more important than how I say it."

Many engineers do not understand that how *they say something is as important and sometimes more important than what they say. They believe that the data speaks for itself. This is simply not the case. If you want to be successful in the long run, if you want to be able to influence others, how you communicate is just as important, if not more important at times, than what you communicate.*

If Career-Limiting Belief #3 Is Part of Your Map of The World...

Throughout your education, you were given examinations to determine what you had learned. The accuracy of your answers determined your grade. And, as an engineering or science student, very often the accuracy of your answer was measured in decimal points or some parameters that were equally unambiguous. Therefore, the *what* of your answers determined your grade; that was the determiner of success. It was easy to believe, simply, that data rules and that it did not matter how you spoke to others.

Influencing others (besides your professors) was not so important in school. Conveying that you had learned what you were expected to learn was your primary purpose. Very often, *how* you communicated the answer to a question, issue, or problem usually did not enter into your response, except perhaps regarding accuracy. How you verbally presented your information, how you verbally interacted with your fellow students, how you wrote your answers—these were not important parameters in most cases.

Scientists now know that when humans communicate, only a small portion of the "connection" between people is generated by the content of what they say [1]. In fact, the major portion of the connection, the openness, and the understanding generated between people in communication are generated by non-verbal behavior. Without an understanding of this portion of the communication process, you will continue to communicate in your organization the same way you communicated in college with your professors and fellow students…as if you were taking an examination. For long-term career success, you must learn new communication protocols.

Career-Limiting Belief #3 Produces an Ineffective Focus of Attention

"Data is more important than people's perceptions."

When you believe that data rules and that you do not have to consider *how* you are communicating that data, your Focus of Attention is very narrow. You look through the world for hard, factual data and essentially ignore communication processes. You ignore the abundant subtle non-verbal feedback that indicates how your audience is responding to the data. Some areas where you may focus your attention as a result of this limiting belief are listed below:

- What are the important data?
- I need to overpower others with information.
- How can I find more information?
- I focus on the data.
- I talk to everyone the same way.
- I do not care if people like what I say or how I say it; the information is what is really important.

This Stance Results in Negative Physiological and Emotional States

Ignoring the delivery method for data is a mistake. And if you are of the mindset that only the data matters, your work will experience indifference or even resistance. If you portray an indifference to the needs of others, expect the same in return.

As for your own perspective, the Focus of Attention questions and statements listed previously will produce certain specific, emotional and physiological responses in you. You will demonstrate:

- A lack of concern for others
- A conceited attitude toward the merit of your analysis, data, or approach
- An intolerance for the questions of others
- A palpable impatience with the questions of others

Holding Onto This Idea Generates Career-Limiting Actions and Behaviors

"I am unwilling to listen to others."

Ultimately, you act, using this negative Map of the World and your Focus of Attention. It's likely that you will do damage to your own reputation if you are unwilling to change. For example, these are some of the actions that clearly represent Limiting Belief #3:

- You are unwilling to listen to others.
- You display impatience when explaining technical information to others.
- You are intolerant with explanations that are not based on data or are not based on *your* data, in particular.
- You purposefully withhold information.

Real World Example: Not Conveying Information Well = Negative Outcomes

Bill is a good engineer. In fact, he is an excellent engineer. However, when he talks to people, he invariably gets to a point in the discussion where his voice tone conveys a very condescending attitude. His frustration increases when people do not seem to understand his information easily.

People tolerate Bill, but they do not like talking to him and when he gets into his condescending attitude, they respond with their own condescending attitude. This creates tension in the discussion and Bill responds by being even more condescending, which increases tensions. Thus, a never-ending negative spiral has made work-related conversations with Bill stressful.

Bill has a difficult time influencing people and getting his ideas implemented. He is very certain that *how* he communicates his ideas has absolutely no impact on his effectiveness. His attitude is that the problem always resides with the other person. Bill is convinced that the information he is conveying is the most important aspect of the conversation and if people do not "get it," he lets them know that he is annoyed. He believes that data alone should be the primary instrument for decision-making. See Figure 11.1.

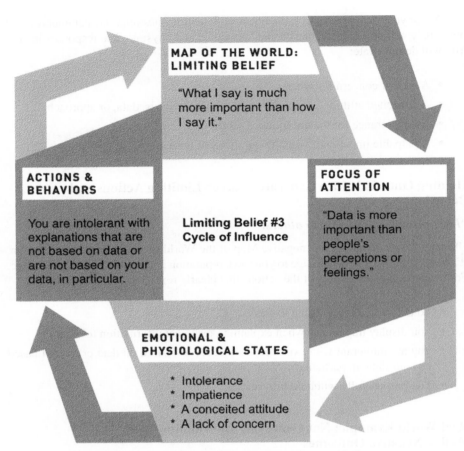

FIGURE 11.1. Career-Limiting Belief #3 Cycle of Influence.

Add Gem of Wisdom #3 to Your Current Map of the World

How you communicate matters: "How I present information often can sway the outcome and influence others more significantly than what information I present. I know that influencing others is dependent upon a strong combination of data and delivery."

Successful technology managers and successful engineers and technologists understand that to many engineers, information, data, and facts, are most important. However, to be truly successful, to actually convince and influence others, you must understand that how ideas and information are presented can often be as important or more important than the actual information itself. This is how we are hard-wired. I do not believe we have a choice in the matter.

Consider the raw information (the knowledge being presented) to be like the data in a database. Consider the way the information is being presented as the data format. If the correct format is not adhered to, the data will not be transmitted accurately. Therefore, the transmission will not be effective. The same holds true for human communication. If the communication process by which the data is presented is not appropriate for the listener, then the message will not be heard, regardless of the facts.

The data format for human communication is the non-verbal portion of the communication process, the context. The actual data in the communication process is the content or the information being transmitted. Therefore, the data we want to communicate to others rides on the non-verbal portion of the communication process, very much like a radio message rides along on a carrier wave. In this way, human communication is a two-part process: the data (the content) and also the context (the process). To be truly effective in the technical world, both must be utilized appropriately.

Adding Gem #3 Produces an Expansive, Positive Shift in Your Focus of Attention

"How is my audience reacting to the information I am presenting?"

By adding the knowledge that the *how* is as important as the *what*, you have tapped into a powerful secret. This insight to your Map of the World will shift your Focus of Attention to the following areas:

- How are others, my listeners, reacting to what I am saying and presenting?
- How does my choice of words compare to the words used by my audience? Should I use different words? Am I targeting by audience correctly?
- How does my voice tone compare to the voice tone used by my audience? Should I use a different voice tone?
- Is my body posture effective in conveying my message to my audience?
- Am I evaluating how my communication is proceeding through observation?
- Am I influencing my audience or just giving them information?

Gem #3 Leads to Useful Physiological and Emotional States

"My communication (i.e., data) is only effective if it is received by others as I intended."

The shift of focus will, in turn, generate new emotional and physiological states that allow you to see that data alone will not always influence others. Your changed perspective will include:

- Curiosity
- Calmness

- A sense of interest in the other person
- A sense of cooperation

Gem #3 Can Lead to Career-Enhancing Actions and Behaviors

"I will control how I communicate so I can control the response I receive."

We have all probably had the experience of communicating an idea and then we get an unexpected response. This is often the result of not understanding that how we communicate is important. You must learn to control your communication delivery as well as your communication content. In fact, the delivery process can often override the content. For most engineers, technical managers, and technologists, data is data, and engineers often expect data itself to simply be enough to convince and influence others. That means that most technical professionals ignore the communication process and rely on the content to be enough to "sell" their ideas.

However, that is not how it works. Once you understand these principals, you will find that you can get much farther in your communication process by altering your delivery than you can by altering your content.

Successful technical people understand the need to be as good at the delivery of content as they are at the generation of that content. Therefore, it is important to learn the tools of effective communication and I am not talking about the graphics of your presentation. I am talking about your verbal and non-verbal communication style. By adopting this Gem of Wisdom, you will be on the way to behaving more effectively in your communication with others. Your new perspective will have wide impact.

Some of the new behaviors you may adopt are:

1. **You will become keenly aware of subtle non-verbal communication cues.**
2. **You will take into account the communication style preferred by your audience.**
3. **You will increase your communication flexibility.**

Let's look at each of these actions and behaviors in more detail to determine how they might shed light on more general behaviors that may develop from this Gem of Wisdom.

1. **You will become keenly aware of subtle non-verbal communication cues.** Most of us believe that communication, real communication, takes place in the words we use, the information we convey, and the data we present. In actuality, communication takes place on a multitude of levels both verbal, non-verbal, and at the level of raw information [1], [2]. Therefore, when most people assume that communication is primarily verbal data transmission, they miss all the various other communication levels that could be informing them regarding the efficacy of their communication process. Adopting Gem of Wisdom #3 will allow you

to be alert to a multitude of communication subtleties that will allow you to enhance the effectiveness of your communication process [2].

2. **You will take into account the communication style preferred by your audience.** People all have a preference for the way they want to be communicated with [2]. Each of us communicates in our own style, and we use that personal default communication style when we communicate with others. That means that as long as we are communicating with people who have preferred styles similar to ours we will have an effective communication process. However, if their preferred communication style is significantly different than our own, we will have a difficult (and perhaps contentious) communication.

    Imagine being able to assess and adjust your own communication style in the moment so as to communicate most effectively with other people. You would be able to expand the universe of people with whom you could effectively communicate and influence.

3. **You will increase your communication flexibility.** A good deal of communication flexibility is necessary for any manager or employee to be truly effective. That means that you are capable of communicating in a style that is most suited to your audience. Rather than adhering to the philosophy that everyone must adapt to your communication style, you should take on the challenge of adjusting your communication style to that of your audience in real-time. For example, you need to have the flexibility to adjust your communication to various people in a meeting rather than communicating with everyone in the same way.

Real World Example: Gem of Wisdom #3 in Action

Bill is a good engineer. In fact, he is an excellent engineer. When Bill talks to people, he understands that getting people to understand his information and his ideas is a complex process and it is his responsibility to help people understand him. He understands that he wants not only to convey data, but to influence others as well. So Bill asks questions of the people he is talking to so that he can understand how they prefer to have information presented to them. He then adjusts his communication style so that it matches their preferred style. By doing this, Bill ensures that people are open and receptive to his messages. In fact, people often agree with Bill and his ideas even if they fundamentally have different views. At the very least, they understand his perspective. Bill has learned the lesson that how a message is conveyed, be it technical or non-technical, is often as important as the content of the message itself.

Bill has also learned one very important corollary to being an effective communicator. He has learned the answer to this question: "Who is responsible for effective communication: the sender, the receiver, or both?" Bill has learned that the person responsible for effective communication is the sender, because the sender is the only person who truly understands the message's intent. It is only the sender who can evaluate if the message has been received the way it was intended. So while it is wonderful to have a good listener in the conversation, and while it also wonderful to have two

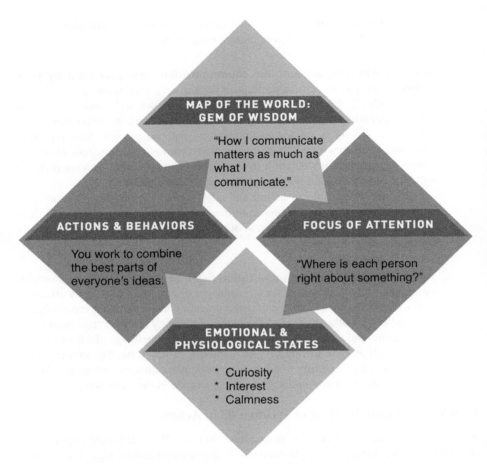

FIGURE 11.2. Career-Enhancing Gem of Wisdom #3 Cycle of Influence.

eager participants in a conversation, it is still the ultimate responsibility of the sender to check, with questions, that the message was received in the way it was intended. See Figure 11.2.

References

[1] A. Pentland, "To Signal Is Human," *American Scientist*, vol. 98, no. 3, pp. 204–211, May–June 2010.

[2] S. Knight, *NLP at Work: The Essence of Excellence (People Skills for Professionals)*, 3rd Edition, Nicholas Brealey Publishing, London, 2009.

Avoiding Shoptalk:
Career-Limiting Belief #4

"I'll avoid the difficult interpersonal conversations long enough for them to just go away."

Engineers generally do not like conflict and will often avoid and delay difficult conversations until those conversations hopefully are no longer necessary. At times, those problems become so big that their complications far exceed anything that would have occurred if addressed earlier. If you want to succeed and achieve a long career as an engineer, scientist, technologist, or as a technical manager, you must become comfortable with conflict and you must ideally learn how to diffuse it before it becomes intense. Diffusing conflict before it grows is the sign of an effective communicator.

If Career-Limiting Belief #4 Is Part of
Your Map of the World...

"I don't like difficult conversations and so I will avoid them."

While some careers, such as the legal profession, require the use of conflict to be successful, the technical world seems to be one in which interpersonal conflict is not so prevalent. Software does not argue. It either works or it does not. Computers either work or they do not. The solution to an equation is either correct or it is not. The universe

The Fully Integrated Engineer: Combining Technical Ability and Leadership Prowess, First Edition. Steven T. Cerri.
© 2016 The Institute of Electrical and Electronics Engineers, Inc. Published 2016 by John Wiley & Sons, Inc.

does not change rules based on who wins an argument. This is the typical world of the engineer. Conflict can be rare when dealing with technology itself. Technology is not arbitrary, emotional, or filled with human conflict. But it is created by, used by, and maintained by humans. And for humans, conflict is a natural part of life.

Engineering is mostly about working with people who use technology. And, like most people, engineers and technologists often attempt to avoid conflict at work, which forces them to put off conversations that may bring conflict. Often, this avoidance tactic does not lead to the situation getting better. Instead, it often leads to the situation getting worse until the difficult conversation can no longer be avoided. And when the conversation is finally initiated, the problem has grown out of proportion. Almost certainly, the problem would have been more easily addressed if the situation had been confronted earlier. But avoidance creates a situation where, often, the conflict becomes so severe that it only reinforces the fear that conflicts are bad and are to be avoided.

That is why, to be truly effective, you must not delay difficult conversations until they become a problem. You must deal with difficult situations as soon as they arise; in this way, you will avoid the complications that will predictably arise by waiting.

Career-Limiting Belief #4 Produces an Ineffective Focus of Attention

"I need to avoid that person."

When you are trying to avoid difficult conversations, your Focus of Attention is on noticing which conversations will be dangerous and how you can avoid them. You will also focus on who you do not want to talk to and how you can avoid those people. You thoughts often run to ideas like these:

- Where could there be conflict?
- Who do I not like? How can I avoid them?
- Who does not like me? How can I avoid them?
- Who have I argued with before?
- I want to avoid all those conversations that could cause me some form of discomfort.

Such Perspectives Result in Negative Physiological and Emotional States

This Focus of Attention produces certain specific negative emotional and physiological responses in you, which you may not even realize. The emotional and physiological states that might be generated are:

- Anxiety
- Fear
- Apprehension
- Anger

Belief #4 Generates Career-Limiting Actions and Behaviors

"I will avoid discussions that could lead to conflict."

Ultimately, the Map of the World that contains Limiting Belief #4 and its associated Focus of Attention produce emotional and physiological states that lead to avoidance actions. These actions limit your daily work effectiveness.

- You will avoid certain people (those with whom you believe you will or may have conflict).
- You will avoid talking to people that make you uncomfortable.
- You will procrastinate.
- You will outwardly agree with people when you inwardly do not agree with them.
- You will say one thing and then do another.

Real World Example: Fear = Negative Outcomes

Susan has just been given responsibility for a new project. Her manager assigned to her several people that she has not worked with before. She does not know how the new people will work out, but she has assurances from her manager that they are good performers.

Within the first two weeks of the project, Susan notices that one of her team members, Kelly, is not performing up to her expectations. Susan suspects that Kelly will not meet her schedule. Susan has not talked to Kelly, or anyone else on the team for that matter, about her detailed schedule performance. So far they have only discussed a few technical matters. Everyone seems to be working up to Susan's standards except Kelly.

Susan decides to wait to see if Kelly will correct her performance on her own. She does not want to seem like a micromanager.

The project continues and Susan suspects that Kelly is behind on her respective tasks but she avoids asking for schedule updates. She assumes that everyone on the team is able to manage his or her individual workload professionally and that Kelly will ultimately deliver her task on time.

Finally, near the end of the task schedules, Susan asks for a schedule status from everyone on the team. Only then does Kelly tell Susan that she cannot make up the work deficit that has accumulated, missing her respective schedule completion date. Susan explodes. She now tells Kelly about the assessment she made months before—that she was not working up to her standards.

Of course, Kelly is surprised and astonished. She has felt all along that she was performing adequately; otherwise Susan would have said something. Kelly is convinced that the problem is that the tasks assigned were too difficult to be completed in the time allotted. Kelly argues, and accusations are made all round and ill feelings result. Susan wonders what she did wrong and why Kelly is such a poor performer. Kelly feels unfairly attacked and thinks Susan is a poor manager. See Figure 12.1.

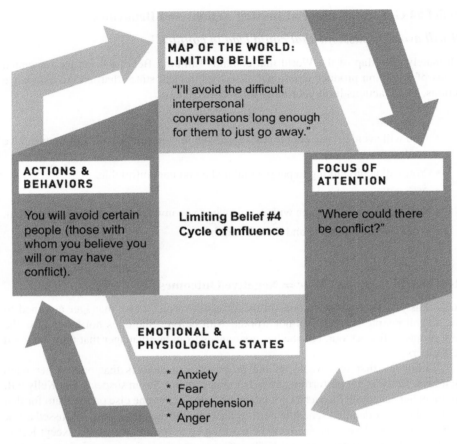

FIGURE 12.1. Career-Limiting Belief #4 Cycle of Influence.

Add Gem of Wisdom #4 to Your Current Map of The World

Do the difficult thing: "I understand that I pay now or I pay later; avoiding conflict is paying later and almost always increases conflict and disagreement."

The successful engineers, scientists, technologists, technical managers understand that nothing comes for free. And conflict is one of those often uncomfortable but necessary requirements of most work environments. Conflict can either be engaged in when it is a potentially small conflict, or one can wait until it is so filled with emotional charge that it is far more confrontational than it would have been.

Following Gem #4 Produces a Positive Shift in Your Focus of Attention

"How can I manage an interaction so it does not become a conflict?"

By addressing uncomfortable conversations without waiting, you will enact positive change in your own work habits and those around you. Your questions and perspectives will shift, perhaps looking like these:

- What do I need to know about the situation to make it progress more smoothly?
- Where is there a potential for conflict later on?
- Where could there be a bottleneck to this project?
- What people or groups do I need to notify about what is happening to avoid a conflict later?
- How can I look at the Big Picture in an attempt to find those points where conflict might arise?
- What is the best way to deal with this now to make processes move more smoothly?
- Who is the best person for me to talk to?

Gem #4 Brings More Useful Physiological and Emotional States

With this Gem added to your Map of the World, you will begin to experience confidence in handling situations at work. With this new Focus of Attention, you will invariably create new and different emotional states, such as these:

- Confidence
- Strength
- Ownership
- Team confidence
- Respect for collaboration

Gem #4 Can Generate Career-Enhancing Actions and Behaviors

"I will engage with people in order to clarify our respective positions so that I can remove any present or future potential conflict."

The truly successful engineer, technical manager, or technologist knows that spending time correcting problems is much less effective, in the long run, than avoiding them in the first place. Therefore, it is most important to deal with adverse situations as they arise rather than waiting or avoiding them. In this way, you can streamline workflow for everyone.

Remember, human systems do not function in the same way mechanical systems do. We have all heard that a chain is only as strong as the weakest link. That is true for a mechanical system. In a human system, however, often the system is as strong as the strongest component because the strongest component can amplify the other components of the system. This means that avoiding a conflict is not as effective as dealing with the weakness and making it neutral or turning it into a strength.

Three of the possible behaviors this Gem of Wisdom, where you address conflict up front are as follows:

1. **You will have a willingness to reach out to those with whom you may have conflict.**

2. **You will have a willingness to work collaboratively with those with whom you have a difference of opinion.**

3. **You will align what you say with what you do.**

Let's review each of these actions and behaviors in more detail and evaluate how they might appear in your organization.

1. **You will have a willingness to reach out to those with whom you may have conflict.** Often when we have a sense that conflict might erupt in a situation, we withdraw our participation. We go silent. A better approach, of course, is to engage with those with whom we might have conflict. That means engaging with curiosity and with a willingness to reach out to others in search of understanding and insight.

    Seldom is any situation as it initially appears. A willingness to reach out, to understand, to uncover underlying perceptions can go a long way to diffusing a situation before it develops into a conflict.

2. **You will have a willingness to work collaboratively with those with whom you have a difference of opinion.** Collaboration is a unique process and one that is used well far too infrequently. Collaboration is an approach that postulates that situations do not have to be win–lose. Nor do they have to be situations where each party has to give up a little of this and a little of that. Collaboration is a process by which no one gives up anything until all parties understand each other's positions well and then all parties seek to attain maximum outcome.

    The goal of collaboration is for all parties to achieve as much as possible of what they want. Sometimes each party gets most of what they each want, and sometimes each party gets only a subset of their wish list. But in collaboration, neither party feels that one has the advantage. This process will invariably diffuse most conflict.

3. **You will align what you say with what you do.** Often, when people attempt to avoid conflict, they will say whatever they feel they must in order to keep peace. Later, it becomes apparent (when their actions are more aligned with how they truly feel) that they did not tell the truth. Often, this will produce a mismatch

between expectations and deliverables, and the result is that others feel betrayed, lied to, and manipulated. You are perceived as deceitful.

A much better approach is to dig deep for your resolve and courage and respectfully speak what is on your mind in an effort to explain, in a collaborative way, what is important to you. This is the first step in collaboration and in ultimately avoiding conflict. And it allows you to spontaneously align what you say with what you do, because your core needs are aligned.

Real World Example: Gem of Wisdom #4 in Action

Susan has just been given responsibility for a new project. Her manager assigned to her several people that she has not worked with before. She does not know how the new people will work out, but she has assurances from her manager that they are good performers.

Within the first two weeks of the project, Susan notices that one of her team members, Kelly, is not performing up to her expectations. Susan suspects that Kelly will not meet her schedule. Susan has not talked to Kelly, or anyone else on the team for that matter, about her detailed schedule performance. So far they have only discussed a few technical matters. Everyone seems to be working up to Susan's standards except Kelly.

Susan decides to take action and have a discussion with her immediately.

She asks Kelly to join her in the conference room for a discussion. Susan first asks Kelly how she thinks her work is progressing. Kelly explains that she thinks she is working just fine. This is important information for Susan. It indicates that Kelly thinks there is not a problem with her performance. This tells Susan that when she conveys her message regarding Kelly's performance, Kelly will be surprised by the information.

Susan diplomatically but clearly explains that each task has been assigned with the expectation that each person will perform at a specific minimum level. She explains that the allotted schedule time was determined based on a reasonable expectation of task performance as well as past performance. Susan indicates that she is concerned with Kelly's progress. She states further that she believes the Kelly may have difficulty completing her task on time. She then asks what Kelly's assessment is. Does she agree with her?

Kelly responds that she does not really understand what Susan is talking about. Kelly believes that she will be able to get the tasks done on time. If it seems that she is a little behind now she is certain she can make up the time later in the schedule.

This gives Susan valuable insight into how Kelly views her work and her progress. Susan explains her expectations and her evaluations. Susan explains further what she expects in terms of attendance in the office, adherence to the schedule, completion of tasks, communication with colleagues, and other important issues. Susan takes this opportunity to explain exactly how she likes to manage and gets feedback from Kelly regarding how she likes to be managed. By the end of this meeting, Susan makes her expectations regarding performance very clear to Kelly and she explains to Kelly that if she needs help, Susan is there to find the resources to assist her in her task. And she emphasizes that waiting too long will make it very difficult for Susan to help. Kelly understands that it is in her best interest and the project's best interest to be honest with Susan regarding her schedule performance.

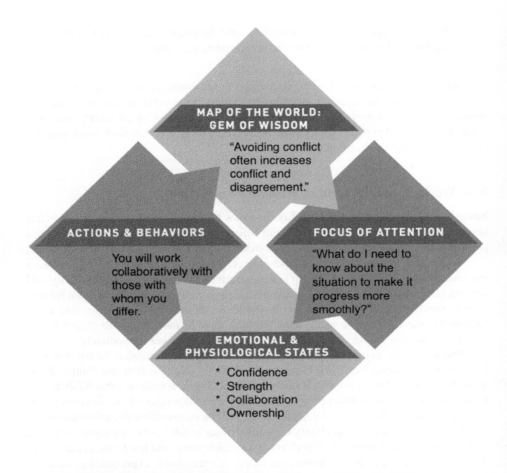

FIGURE 12.2. Career-Enhancing Gem of Wisdom #4 Cycle of Influence.

Kelly is not completely happy with this discussion. However, she now understands what Susan expects of her. Susan has made it very clear that she expects the project to be completed on schedule and with no excuses. She has also made it clear that it is better for Kelly to ask for help than to miss her schedule. She sets up a feedback and oversight process with Kelly so that Susan can provide weekly feedback regarding Kelly's performance and, in turn, Kelly can provide Susan with a weekly schedule and performance status. Kelly does not like this arrangement; she feels micromanaged. But Susan has made it clear–this is how they will work together going forward.

By the time the meeting is over Kelly understands that if she is to gain more operational freedom on her future tasks, she will have to earn that freedom by performing to Susan's standards. See Figure 12.2.

13

I'll Do My Own Work: Career-Limiting Belief #5

"I assume my coworkers are professionals and will do their jobs well, so I'll stick to my own work."

Engineers and other technical professionals, like many others, take a great deal of pride in doing their jobs very well, and they often believe everyone else will do their jobs well, too. Therefore, they tend to avoid the appearance of being nosy or prying when it comes to the work tasks of others. However, knowing what others are doing and how their own work impacts the work of others might prevent problems and unforeseeable consequences. But since many engineers assume coworkers will behave professionally and will do their job well, they avoid vital conversations. For your long-term career growth, you must learn that your success is dependent upon the success of others (and the reverse is also true).

If Career-Limiting Belief #5 Is Part of Your Map of the World...

Most technical professionals take the "professional" part of their title very seriously. They intend to be professional, and they expect the same from others, as well. This desire and expectation for professionalism lead most engineers, especially those given

The Fully Integrated Engineer: Combining Technical Ability and Leadership Prowess, First Edition. Steven T. Cerri.
© 2016 The Institute of Electrical and Electronics Engineers, Inc. Published 2016 by John Wiley & Sons, Inc.

responsibility early in their careers for the management of others, to avoid checking in with colleagues out of a sense of respect. It also allows people to bury their heads in their own work, avoiding a show of interest in the work of others unless absolutely necessary.

These approaches are often mistakes. You cannot assume that everyone will perform to an acceptable level of professionalism. You cannot assume that everyone will do his or her job as might be expected and/or desired.

Most new technical managers or team leads wait until something goes wrong before they check to see how things are progressing. They do not want to micromanage others or appear to interfere in the work of their colleagues, so they wait until it is very late in the schedule to review task progress or ask questions. Often, it is at this late date that problems become apparent.

It is important to understand that if you are managing people or you are working as part of a team, an essential task in the workflow is to monitor the progress of others appropriately, asking questions in order to understand the impact of the work of others on you and the project as a whole.

Understanding how much to insert yourself into the work of others is not a black-and-white process. It takes judgment and finesse. But it must be done.

Career-Limiting Belief #5 Produces an Ineffective Focus of Attention

"I will just do my own individual work."

When we believe that everyone is a professional, we allow ourselves to overlook potential problems, either in ourselves or with others. Ignoring the struggles of coworkers is not professional behavior, as the essence of professionalism is sharing responsibility and knowledge. And understanding what your colleagues are doing is not being nosy. By allowing yourself to ignore what others are doing, you may be focusing your attention of the following ideas and areas:

- I will just do my work, and others will do their work.
- I do not want to be perceived as micromanaging or interfering with someone else's tasks.
- I do not want people to check on me, so I will not check on them.
- I really do not want to know what other people are doing because it does not really matter to my work.
- We each have our own tasks to do. I am sure they will do their work just fine.

Focusing Your Attention on These Ideas Results in Unproductive Physiological and Emotional States

"I fear being perceived as nosy or as a micromanager."

This Focus of Attention will produce negative emotional and physiological states. Some of the generated states that can be expected might look like these:

- You have a deep desire for privacy.
- You feel an overdeveloped sense of task ownership.

- You feel threatened by too much communication with others.
- You fear divulging too much about your work, because divulging too much makes you feel less essential.

These Emotional and Physiological States Generate Career-Limiting Actions and Behaviors

"I will avoid asking people how their work is progressing."

Ultimately, your Map of the World and your Focus of Attention generate ways of working that impede your career's progress. Some of the actions that clearly represent Limiting Belief #5 might look like these.

- You avoid finding out what other people are doing.
- You ask for status and information only when necessary.
- You avoid the appearance of micromanaging others.
- You wait until people volunteer information rather than asking them for anything.
- You withhold information.

Real World Example: Not Engaging = Negative Outcomes

Mark has just been promoted to task leader. His cross-functional team is composed of three programmers from his department and two electrical engineers, on loan, from another department. He has responsibility for a software and hardware program with a schedule of six months. Since this is his first management/lead position, he has been given the typical work structure of a first-time lead: half-time manager/lead and half-time individual-contributor/programmer.

As is often the case in these situations, Mark assumes that he is managing professional people like himself. As such, he feels that he does not have to actually manage his team members very much. He knows that he would not want to be managed very closely if the situation were reversed. So he does his own programming half time. He talks regularly to his fellow programmers on the team, since he knows them and they are all programmers. He further assumes that the electrical engineers understand the requirements as presented to them and are professionals and will do the work as requested. This leads Mark to assume that the electrical engineers are progressing as planned and if they have any problems they will alert Mark.

Since this is a six-month project and Mark does not want to be perceived as a micromanager, he plans on only three status meetings; the first is the kick-off meeting, the second is a status meeting at three months, and the final status meeting is to occur two weeks before project completion.

The kick-off meeting seems to be a great meeting. Everyone is on board. Mark does not ask many detailed questions because he does not want to appear to be micromanaging. He regards his colleagues as professionals, and they are. Some of them, in fact, have more experience than Mark. And Mark is certainly not an electrical engineer, so what valid questions can he ask the two electrical engineers? He assumes they will do their work and all will be well.

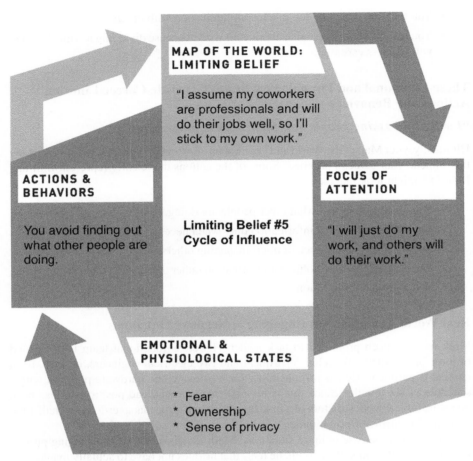

FIGURE 13.1. Career-Limiting Belief #5 Cycle of Influence.

The three-month meeting seems to indicate that everyone is doing just fine. Mark and his three programmers are all doing well. Their work is coming along on schedule and the two electrical engineers are indicating that their work is progressing also. Mark is happy and satisfied that he is being a good manager.

Two weeks before the end of the project, Mark convenes the final meeting. His software team is now ready for integration with the hardware, but the hardware team is not ready. The electrical engineers tell Mark that their manager called them off the project for several weeks. As a consequence they have lost some critical time. They have only recently been put back on Mark's project by their manager and will need an additional month to complete the project. Mark's tactic of treating everyone as a professional has resulted in a failed project. See Figure 13.1.

Add Gem of Wisdom #5 to Your Current Map of the World

Professionals engage: "Most engineers and technologists want to do a good job. But I understand that everyone's definition of good is not the same."

Successful technical managers, engineers, and technologists know that everyone has different capabilities, competencies, and standards. Assuming otherwise courts disaster. Therefore, you must understand that leaving people alone to do their work is not the height of excellent management. It is a signal of avoidance and ineffective leadership.

Adding Gem #5 Enables a Positive Shift in Your Focus of Attention

"Does anyone need my help? Is everyone doing well? Are we all moving in the same direction?"

Knowing that professional and personal standards can vary widely will shift your Focus of Attention. Your new perspectives might include these new ways of questioning or investigating work patterns:

- How does what I do impact others?
- How does what others do impact me?
- How does everyone's work come together to make this a complete and successful project?
- How can I help others?
- What do I need to know about the work of others in order for the project to succeed?
- Are we all working with the same assumptions?
- Are we all communicating to the level necessary for success?

Gem #5 Will Result in Effective Physiological and Emotional States

Once again, the power of curiosity will save the day. Gem #5 will generate very useful emotional and physiological states:

- Curiosity
- Patience
- Confidence
- A desire to coordinate efforts

- A willingness to be helpful
- An interest in supporting others

Gem of Wisdom #5 Will Generate Career-Enhancing Actions and Behaviors

"I will learn to appropriately ask questions and engage in conversations and exchanges that share pertinent information."

The successful engineer, technical manager, and technologist understands that the most important determinant to a successful long-term career is the context (in other words, the structure of communication within the organization). Therefore, success requires agile and perceptive levels of communication, sharing, oversight, and review, all of which are necessary to ensure that the work will be performed well.

Below are three possible behaviors this Gem of Wisdom might generate in you:

1. **You will withhold judgment until you have asked questions to gather information.**

2. **You are comfortable asking questions because you are generally uncertain that you truly understand what someone has told you.**

3. **You engage with people and are curious as to what "makes them tick," figuring out what is important to them and why.**

Let's dig a little deeper into each of these actions and behaviors to determine how they might show up in your organization.

1. **You will withhold judgment until you have asked questions to gather information.** It is said that first impressions are important. What is often not said is that first impressions are often wrong. Think about it. How many times have you thought upon first meeting someone that he/she would become a good friend, only to later determine that it's not true? Maybe someone you thought was a jerk turned out to be your best friend. First impressions can be misleading. So, withholding judgment will ensure that you will not make a snap judgment and you will not have to backtrack on a decision.

   The key behavior that will allow you to withhold judgment is your willingness to ask questions. With respect and with authentic curiosity, attempt to understand what is important to others and how their work is progressing.

2. **You are comfortable asking questions because you are generally uncertain that you truly understand what someone has told you.** We use language to convey information. What is often not in our conscious awareness is that we give meaning to words with the assumption that everyone gives the same meaning to those same words. This is clearly not the case. Often, words that mean something to us mean something slightly different or very different to others. If we are aware of this possibility, we will be less apt to assume we

understand what other people mean. This uncertainty about meaning will lead you to question others in an attempt to clarify. This process of questioning is crucial to effective communication.

3. **You engage with people and are curious as to what "makes them tick," figuring out what is important to them and why.** Each of us has different values, beliefs, and motives. These all lead to different behaviors. Here is a key idea: *if you want to change behaviors, do not focus on the behaviors.* By being curious about a person's Map of the World and Focus of Attention, you can achieve effective communication and respectful influence.

Real World Example: Gem of Wisdom #5 in Action

Mark has just been promoted to task leader. His cross-functional team is composed of three programmers from his department and two electrical engineers, on loan, from another department. He has responsibility for a software and hardware program with a schedule of six months. Since this is his first management/lead position, he has been given the typical work structure of a first-time lead: half-time manager/lead and half-time individual-contributor/programmer.

As is often the case in these situations, Mark knows that he would like to assume that he is managing professional people like himself. But he knows this is a recipe for disaster. He is not assuming that people are incompetent, only that they probably perceive the world differently than does Mark. So Mark decides that he will have to manage his team closely, especially the two electrical engineers who are on loan to his project and may not be as devoted to their project tasks as Mark and his programmers are to theirs.

He knows that each person has a slightly different definition of what it means to be a professional and that each team member may have a different sense of responsibility to their task, their manager, Mark's project, and their department. Therefore, Mark calls a meeting with all his team members. He tells them that while they are all professionals, they are also dependent upon each other at every juncture of the project.

Therefore, Mark tells the team there will be weekly status meetings. Although some may feel that conducting weekly meetings is excessive, this project depends on good communication between two very different departments. The communication must be close and open to ensure success.

At the weekly meetings, it will be important for each team member to review and explain individual tasks in detail, including assumptions made, interface parameters developed, current status of the work, and potential issues. They also need to address any requests from other team members. It is important for each member to understand what the others are doing, and Mark pushes for the disclosure of detail in these weekly meetings. While everyone is a professional, this is no time for territoriality. In six months the code must be written, tested, integrated with the hardware being developed by the electrical engineers, and tested again. This will be an intimate and open process. The team members understand and accept the structure.

At the weekly status meeting at the beginning of the fourth month, the electrical engineers tell Mark that their manager has taken them off his project to work on a higher priority project. He listens to the electrical engineers but does not attempt to change their minds or their priorities; Mark knows they are merely taking direction from their manager. They are not the decision-makers in this case.

After the meeting, Mark goes to discuss this change of priorities with the manager of the electrical engineering department. The manager of the electrical engineers is adamant that Mark's project must be secondary to the new priority put forth by the electrical engineering manager. He cannot argue with the manager, so Mark goes to his manager for help. Mark asks his manager to talk to the electrical engineering manager to determine if Mark's project can be moved up the priority list.

Mark's manager returns to him indicating that the new priorities must stand because the new priority is important to the overall company, not just to any one department. Mark's manager adjusts the project schedule by allocating an additional two months to complete the task. Mark can now move forward advising his team that priorities and schedules have changed, still leading to success.

See Figure 13.2.

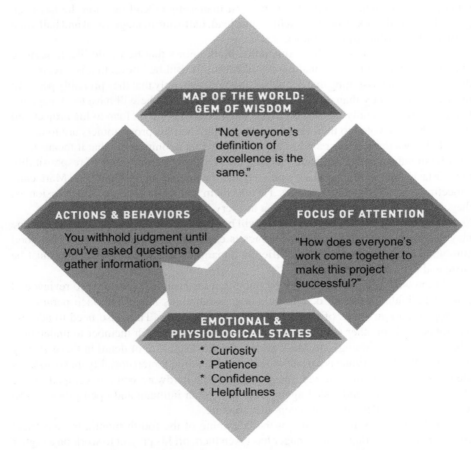

FIGURE 13.2. Career-Enhancing Gem of Wisdom #5 Cycle of Influence.

14

Ducking Delegation:
Career-Limiting Belief #6

"I love my technical work. If I delegate and the person runs into trouble, I will just pick up the pieces myself."

Most engineers, new technical managers, and technologists do not know how to delegate or how to have others delegate to them. This is a key skill in your advancement. Learn to delegate effectively and you will find that success will come much easier.

If Career-Limiting Belief #6 Is Part of
Your Map of the World...

Very often, engineers do not know how to delegate or how to have others delegate to them. In reality, once they are given a task or an assignment, they are accustomed to working on their own, in their own way. They are what is known as *individual contributors*.

The Fully Integrated Engineer: Combining Technical Ability and Leadership Prowess, First Edition. Steven T. Cerri.
© 2016 The Institute of Electrical and Electronics Engineers, Inc. Published 2016 by John Wiley & Sons, Inc.

As well, there is an art of being delegated *to*. When professionals understand how to assist others in delegating to them, they find that they are more effective and successful. However, too often, when people are given a task that includes delegating to others, they balk. Instead, they keep the task for themselves, increasing their own workload. If they could learn to delegate effectively, they would be able to accomplish a great deal more and they would be more effective.

Your goal is to learn how to assist others on both sides of the delegation activity. Doing so will allow you to be more effective and maximize your results, the results of your manager, and the results of your organization. Understanding delegation and the process of delegation is important whether you are an individual contributor, a lead, or a manager.

Career-Limiting Belief #6 Fosters an Ineffective Focus of Attention

"I can just do this myself."

Generally, engineers, technologists, and new technical managers have difficulty delegating because of past training in school and work. Many of the limiting beliefs presented in the previous chapters reveal patterns and mind sets that reflect those old patterns: "I know the right answer, and I could easily do this work myself." When a technical lead or manager delegates, often the feeling is "I am just giving this task to someone else because I just do not have the time to do it myself. And if they start and cannot finish or have some difficulty, I will just have to find the extra time and do it myself." This generates an entire set of false Focus of Attention stances, as follows:

- If another person's task is in trouble, how can I help fix it?
- Under what circumstances can I work a few extra hours and help out if necessary?
- I do not want my boss to know that the project is in trouble, so I will fix it myself.
- How can I just work a little harder so I can put the project back on track?

These Stances Result in Negative Physiological and Emotional States

"I fear that other people are not as competent as I am."

The Focus of Attention statements listed above will produce certain specific, physiological and emotional responses in you, most of which are based in fear. A fear of delegation might be grounded in a fear of looking incapable to perform a task. Some of the states you might experience are:

- Hesitancy
- Fear
- Uncertainty as to what to do
- Anxiety

Staying in this Mindset Generates Career-Limiting Actions and Behaviors

"I will jump into a task rather than manage the problem."

Ultimately, your Map of the World and your Focus of Attention produce emotional and physiological states that negatively contribute to your work habits. If you cannot master the art of delegating, these are some of the ineffective results that you may see:

- You will jump into fixing a task without completely evaluating your alternatives.
- When a task is in trouble, you will think of lending a hand instead of looking for other resources.
- You will distrust everyone's work except your own.
- You will work longer and longer hours.
- Your meetings will become more combative.

Real World Example: No Delegating = Negative Outcomes

Note: By my definition, managers do not do any individual technical work. Rather, they spend all their time managing the work of others. Project leads usually lead a project or task where they allocate part of their time performing technical work and part of their time performing management work. The project lead has no hire/fire authority over the people they lead. Project leads are identical to technical leads in this discussion.

Sally is a new technical lead. She has been given lead responsibility on a part-time basis. Part of the time, Sally manages a team of two employees, and the remainder of the time she is expected to contribute her technical expertise as an individual contributor. A schedule has been developed in coordination with her team members and her manager. Everything is set. Sally wants to do a good job since this is her first assignment as a lead. She wants to impress her manager and she wants to continue being promoted into higher management positions.

She is watching her team members closely. Part way through the project schedule, one of her team members, Bill, tells Sally that his task has fallen behind schedule. He has been working weekends for some time in an effort to bring his task back on schedule, but it has not worked. She now has to decide what to do.

She does not want her manager to think she is unqualified for management, and so she decides not to tell her manager anything about the potential schedule impact. She instead decides to help Bill with his task while continuing to perform her lead duties plus her individual contributor duties. This will require that she work weekends for a while in the hope that she can help put Bill's task back on schedule. Her thought is that with both she and Bill working weekends they can put his task back on schedule.

Unfortunately, even with Sally and Bill working weekends Bill's task remains problematic. Ultimately, she has to tell her manager that the task is hopelessly behind schedule and it is actually too late in the program to get additional resources to help. Sally has to extend the scheduled completion date of the project by a month. Her manager is not happy. See Figure 14.1.

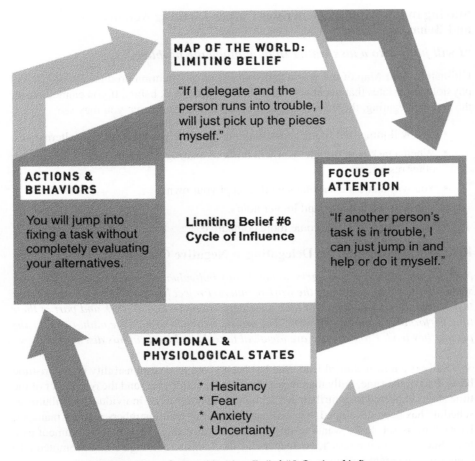

FIGURE 14.1. Career-Limiting Belief #6 Cycle of Influence.

Add Gem of Wisdom #6 to Your Current Map of the World

"I understand that management is about managing resources; it's not about doing the engineering tasks."

Many engineers, technologists, and technical professionals who are given a task or team lead or management position believe their primary job is to do tasks along with other technical members of the team. In the early stages of being a team leader, this may be true. However, when tasks or projects get into trouble, many new leads or managers think that the best way to fix a problem situation is just to work harder. They will work an extra weekend or they will jump right in and help get the project back on track.

However, the manager's job is not, generally, to work weekends contributing their technical capabilities to fix the situation. It is not the manager's job or the project lead's job to take on more individual contributor work in order to alleviate the difficulty. Instead, often the job is to evaluate the situation and to find more resources or reallocate more resources in order to fix the situation as necessary. As a lead or manager, when a task or project is at risk, you are expected to manage the task or project back to health, not to do the work yourself.

Adding Gem #6 Enables an Expansive Shift in Your Focus of Attention

"What resources can I use if a problem arises?"

Welding this Gem of Wisdom to your Map will help you to refocus. You will see opportunities anew, such as these:

- How is everyone performing regarding individual, specific tasks?
- All our work should be an "open book."
- Where are the potential risks of the project?
- What resources might I tap, if necessary?
- How can I bring added resources to the task if we get behind schedule?
- Who currently needs or may need my help?

Gem #6 Brings Forth Useful Physiological and Emotional States

The shift of focus will, in turn, generate new emotional and physiological states that allow for your newfound confidence to gain traction in your organization.

- Curiosity
- Confidence in planning
- Confidence with task schedules
- Confidence with resource allocations
- Confidence alerting you manger as to status
- Confidence alerting all team members regarding status

Gem #6 Creates Career-Enhancing Actions and Behaviors

"I should focus on bringing resources to bear on a problem and managing the problem to resolution."

Delegation is as much an art as it is a skill. That is why it is so difficult to do it well. Do you know how to delegate? Do you know how to decide whom to delegate to and how much of the task to delegate and how much to keep for yourself? Do you know how much oversight to provide to a given employee and the given task?

There are specific processes you can use to determine whom to delegate to, how much work to give away, how much work to keep, and how to monitor so the person you delegate to does not feel you are micromanaging. To be able to balance the delegation process with the oversight process is an important success factor. Learn to delegate well and you can expand your sphere of influence significantly. This is one of the cornerstones of successful management and leadership.

By adding the Gem of Wisdom #6 to your Map of the World, you will generate new behaviors, perhaps like these:

1. **You will monitor, closely, the status of all tasks.**
2. **You will instruct team members to notify you immediately of any potential problems.**
3. **You will play scenarios in your mind as to what resources you will tap and what actions you will take if your team encounters difficulty completing assigned tasks.**

Let's look at each of these actions and behaviors in more detail to determine how they might show up in your organization.

1. **You will monitor, closely, the status of all tasks.** Rather than being so fearful of being labeled a micromanager, you will clearly state to your team that your job is to ensure that the project and the associated tasks are completed correctly and on time. To do so, you will need detailed and timely information regarding the status of the tasks so that you can bring additional resources and knowledge to bear if a team member experiences difficulty. With this approach, everyone on the team understands that open communication is a requirement for success.

2. **You will instruct team members to notify you immediately of any potential problems.** While open communication is a critical component of project success, you as the lead or manager, cannot know everything. The person actually performing the task is the most knowledgeable one regarding how the task is progressing. Make it clear to the team that each member is responsible for alerting everyone to any potential difficulties as soon as they have an inkling that difficulty may arise.

3. **You will play out scenarios in your mind as to what resources you will tap and what actions you would take if your team experiences any difficulty completing assigned tasks.** You understand that projects can and do experience

FIGURE 14.2. Career-Enhancing Gem of Wisdom #6 Cycle of Influence.

difficulty. Therefore, you assess what resources you have available in the event of a project problem. You talk to your manager about what resources he or she might make available to you if needed. You mentally strategize what you might do in case a difficult situation or an adverse impact to a task develops. These assessments, discussions, and mental scenarios prepare you for potential adverse situations that may arise.

Real World Example: Gem of Wisdom #6 in Action

Sally is a new technical lead. She has been given lead responsibility on a part-time basis. Part of the time, Sally manages a team of two employees, and the remainder of the time she is expected to contribute her technical expertise as an individual contributor. A schedule has been developed in coordination with her team members and her manager.

Everything is set. Sally wants to do a good job since this is her first assignment as a lead. She wants to impress her manager and she wants to continue being promoted into higher management positions.

She is watching her team members closely. Part way through the project schedule, one of her team members, Bill, tells Sally that his task has fallen behind schedule. He has decided to work weekends to attempt to bring his task back on schedule. Sally is monitoring his progress closely.

After several weeks Sally decides that, even though Bill thinks he can bring his task back on schedule, Sally is not so sure. She decides to intervene. She draws up a recovery plan for Bill's task that includes another engineer from another department on a half-time basis. He is not happy with another person joining him, but Sally makes it clear that this is not Bill's choice; it is her choice.

She presents this plan to her manager along with a request for another person on a half-time basis. Sally's manager is disappointed that the task is behind schedule, but she appreciates the heads up. Because it is critical that the project is completed on time, Sally's manager approves her request.

Sally closely manages the new part-time employee along with Bill to ensure that the task recovers and after three weeks Bill's task is back on schedule and the half-time engineer leaves the project.

She has learned a very valuable lesson. When you are a lead or manager and your project encounters difficulty, the manager's job is to "manage" the project out of trouble. See Figure 14.2.

15

I'll Do What I Like:
Career-Limiting Belief #7

"I want to do what interests me, not necessarily what is strategically important."

Most engineers and technologists and even some leads and managers would rather do what they find interesting, not necessarily what is strategically important to the task, the organization, or the larger outcome. This is generally a common human behavior. If you want to advance, however, there will be many uninteresting tasks along the way. You may also be asked to completely change your job description and your focus. Do the uninteresting tasks, as well as you do what interests you, and you will be successful.

If Career-Limiting Belief #7 Is Part of
Your Map of the World...

"You will avoid tasks that you do not enjoy and you will focus on what you like to do."

Generally speaking, engineers and other technologists love their technical work and they love technology. And because of this interest, they tend to do what they find enjoyable and interesting, not necessarily what is strategically important to their project or their

---

company. But every job is composed of the good and the not-so-good, of the interesting and the not-so-interesting. If you want to be successful in the long run, it is important that you do what you find compelling as well as those less-exciting tasks necessary to the overall project and the company.

Career-Limiting Belief #7 Produces an Ineffective Focus of Attention

"What can I do that I like to do?"

When you are thinking about what you would *rather do*, as opposed to what needs to be done, your vision is out of focus. You are probably thinking thoughts like these:

- What can I do that I like to do?
- What can I do that is fun and interesting?
- How can I do what I want while ignoring what I do not want to do?
- I want to put this uninteresting task off for as long as I can.

Career-Limiting Belief #7 Quickly Leads to Unproductive Physiological and Emotional States

The Focus of Attention questions listed above will produce certain specific, emotional, and physiological responses in you. Some of the states that might be generated are:

- Excitement (… toward what you like to do)
- Curiosity (… about those things that interest you)
- Avoidance (… of those tasks you do not like)
- Boredom (… toward those tasks you do not like to do)

Career-Limiting Belief #7 Promotes Poor Actions and Behaviors

"I will avoid important but undesirable tasks."

Ultimately, your Map of the World and your Focus of Attention generate negative emotional and physiological states that generate the impetus for action. Some of the actions that manifest due to Limiting Belief #7 are these:

- You will avoid important but undesirable tasks.
- You will appear to procrastinate regarding important tasks you should do.
- You will appear not to take direction well.
- You will appear to ignore tasks that others believe are yours to do.

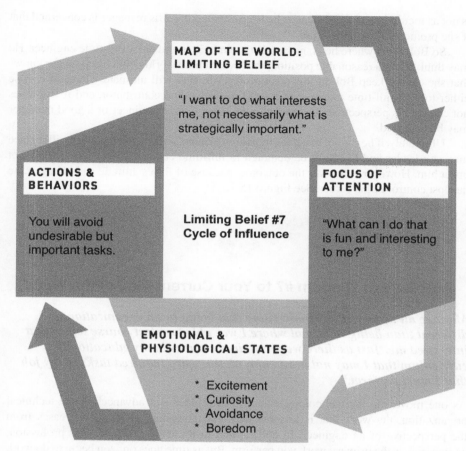

FIGURE 15.1. Career-Limiting Belief #7 Cycle of Influence.

Real World Example: Avoiding What is Necessary = Negative Outcomes

Bob has been a technical lead/entry-level manager for several years. He seems to do a decent job, but he has not been promoted beyond lead/entry-level manager. On the projects he manages, he works as an individual technical contributor at a half-time level and the remainder of the time he works as a project lead.

However, Bob does not seem to focus much on the management portion of his job. He delivers weekly status reports to his manager, but the reports often are not complete. He does not conduct regular meetings with this staff. His management and status meetings with his team are often "spur-of-the-moment" and not well organized.

However, Bob's technical work is excellent. As an individual contributor, he is an excellent engineer. It is clear to his manager that Bob prefers to do the engineering work and only reluctantly focuses on the management issues. Bob's manager has been hesitant to promote him to a full-time management position because it is clear that Bob is not as focused on management as he is on engineering. His manager is concerned that if she promotes Bob, he will fail.

So Bob stays where he is, not a full-time manager and not a full-time engineer. He may think this is a reasonable position, the "best of both worlds," but his manager knows that she cannot keep Bob in this position forever. Bob will ultimately have to choose either to be a full-time manager or a full-time individual contributor, and if Bob does not change his perspective, his reputation as either a good engineer or a good manager may be damaged.

Ultimately, if he cannot make the transition to management, his manager will replace him as a leader and Bob will be demoted to full-time engineer. This may or may not upset him. However, whatever the outcome, because of Bob's attitude and behavior, he has lost control of his career. See Figure 15.1.

Add Gem of Wisdom #7 to Your Current Map of the World

Manage all tasks well: "I understand that being in an organization is different than being in school where I was able to select course topics that interested me. Just as there were required courses in my educational curriculum that I may not have enjoyed, there are required tasks in my job that I must perform."

As one moves up the technology management ladder and advances in the technical organization, the work that is less fun and less interesting generally increases from the perspective of an engineer. In college and in the early years of your profession, engineering is the primary work you perform. But as time goes on, you begin to do work that is not engineering but is necessary as a result of your increased responsibility. This only increases as you advance up the technology management ladder.

If you want to be successful as a technical manager or as an engineer in the long term, performing these less interesting, but necessary, tasks will be important. It just comes with the territory.

Gem of Wisdom #7 Allows for an Expansive Shift in Your Focus of Attention

"What are the most important tasks that must be done for project success?"

Adding this Gem of Wisdom to your map will shift your Focus of Attention to the following:

- What are the most important tasks to the company?
- What are the next important tasks on the project?

- How do I perform those tasks that will make the biggest difference to my company and my team?
- What tasks have the greatest return on investment (ROI)?

Gem #7 Will Result in More Useful Physiological and Emotional States

The shift of focus, in turn, will generate new emotional and physiological states. Some are listed below:

- Curiosity
- Seriousness
- Professionalism
- Discipline

Gem of Wisdom #7 Will Generate Career-Enhancing, Positive Actions and Behaviors

"I focus on the organization's most important tasks, those with high Return On Investment for the work performed."

An easy way to focus on what needs to be done is to constantly drive for the major ROI. Focus on those tasks that move the team, the project, and the organization toward the necessary and desired outcomes, toward the greatest ROI or the greatest return on invested effort. If you focus on the best ROI, you will perform those tasks that do not interest you as well as those that do. Those tasks that do not interest you but move the team toward the greatest ROI may be the most important from the company's point of view. And that is good for you because you will be noticed for doing what needs to be done.

By adding Gem of Wisdom #7 to your Map of the World, you will generate new behaviors, such as these:

1. **You will perform tasks that have a significant impact on those around you.**
2. **You will perform tasks on time.**
3. **People will see you as a model of good leadership.**

Let's look at each of these actions and behaviors in more detail to determine how they might appear in an organization.

1. **You will perform tasks that have a significant impact on those around you.** When you do only the tasks that primarily interest you, by default, you are having an impact on those areas that are usually close to you. When you choose to perform tasks that have a high ROI for your organization, by definition, you are performing tasks that have far reaching impact on those around you.

2. **You will perform tasks on time.** Doing only or primarily what you like means you are procrastinating on those tasks you do not like. Therefore, they are often

late. Being proactive on all categories of tasks means that, in most cases, your work is completed on time.

3. **People will see you as a model of good leadership.** Performing tasks that have the highest ROI for the organization is, in many ways, the definition of leadership. As you move the organization toward the important outcomes you will be seen as a leader.

Real World Example: Gem of Wisdom #7 in Action

Bob has been an engineering lead/manager for several years. He seems to do a decent job, but he has not been promoted beyond task lead/entry-level manager. On the projects he manages, he works as an individual technical contributor at a half-time level and the remainder of the time he works as a project lead.

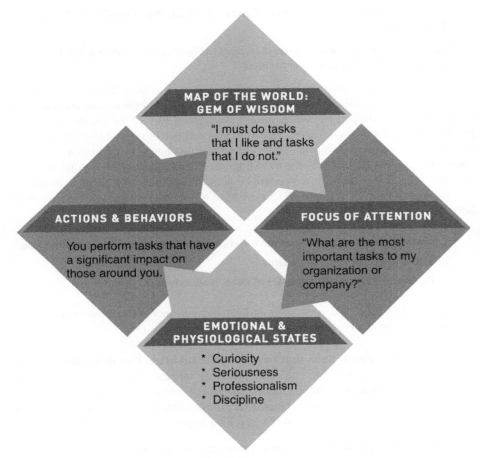

FIGURE 15.2. Career-Enhancing Gem of Wisdom #7 Cycle of Influence.

Bob has decided that it is important for him to make a decision. He wants to advance his career but functioning as a half-time individual contributor and half-time lead is not what he had in mind. He has been discussing his career with his manager, and his manager agrees that Bob must make a decision.

Bob must decide either to be a full-time engineer or set his course to become a full-time manager, because he knows being a half-time individual contributor and half-time manager is a land of limbo.

Bob has decided to set a course to become a full-time manager. This means that while he may, at times, enjoy performing classic engineering work, he knows that the management portion of his work will ensure his career advancement. So Bob spends time preparing for his management meetings. He schedules and conducts regular management meetings with his team. They are extensively scheduled and structured, with agendas, action items, and brief minutes. His weekly status reports to his manager are complete and detailed. Bob has realized that because he made the decision to be a manager, he must change his focus of attention toward those items that are important to his success as a manager. He has decided to leave the engineering tasks to others and his actions demonstrate this decision. He does not jump in with an answer when a problem arises, but facilitates a discussion between the people who are doing the work. They come up with the solution.

At first this approach makes Bob feel that he is being paid for not doing anything important. In the past, being paid meant he was an engineer solving engineering problems. Now he has to adjust his thinking to encompass the fact that the company is now paying him to ensure that other engineers are doing the engineering. His engineering knowledge allows him to understand the details, when necessary, but his managerial perspective allows him to see the larger system and how his projects fit into a larger scheme. See Figure 15.2.

16

Inconsiderate Communication: Career-Limiting Belief #8

"I do not want to change myself just to talk to non-technical people."

Many engineers, technical managers, and technologists do not know how to bridge the gap between themselves and people who do not have their particular specialized expertise. They expect others to make the effort to understand them. To become most effective as someone with specific technical expertise, it is important that you take on the responsibility of being understood.

If Career-Limiting Belief #8 Is Part of Your Map of the World...

"I'm not going to change my communication style to accommodate non-technical people."

Engineers, technical managers, and technologists often do not know how to communicate with others outside their field of expertise. To the non-technical person, the language of technical experts can often sound like a completely different language. Even worse, maybe the listener feels that the technical person is from a different planet, cannot relate

The Fully Integrated Engineer: Combining Technical Ability and Leadership Prowess, First Edition. Steven T. Cerri.
© 2016 The Institute of Electrical and Electronics Engineers, Inc. Published 2016 by John Wiley & Sons, Inc.

to regular humans, and has a condescending attitude toward others who do not have the same areas of expertise or experience.

As engineers, we know how to talk to other engineers, especially those in our own specialized area. Unfortunately, no one taught us how to talk to non-techie folks or people with other areas of expertise. You must learn to communicate with anyone so that you can have the influence and the impact that is necessary to implement and utilize your knowledge and capability.

Many of the significant decisions that are made in the world are not made by technical people, but rather by non-technical people, including legal or financial experts, medical experts, or politicians. Often significant decisions in our own organizations are made by non-technical managers, or financial and legal experts. They are all part of the extensive team that gets things done in the world. Non-technical people who are considering and assessing technical information make many of the important decisions that affect our daily lives both in and outside our immediate organizations. If you cannot communicate with and influence these non-technical decision-makers, then decisions will be made without you.

Career-Limiting Belief #8 Produces an Ineffective Focus of Attention

"My audience has to adjust to me."

When you are thinking that your mindset is the only correct one, your Focus of Attention is that you are right and everyone else is wrong. It also means that you believe (mistakenly) that it is the responsibility of others to change or "get up to speed" in order to understand you. Your world is a very self-centered one, and you are unwilling or incapable of helping others understand. Therefore, your Map of the World puts your Focus of Attention here:

- How am I smarter than these people?
- They just don't get it. They need to understand how this works.
- They don't know what I know. They should just trust me.
- Where are these people ignorant compared to what I know?
- Where can I show them how much I know?

Such Stances Produce Negative Physiological and Emotional States

Working with the ineffective Focus of Attention noted above produces emotional and physiological states that lead to a breakdown in communication. Some of the states you might experience are:

- Arrogance
- Overconfidence
- Unwarranted urgency
- Defensiveness
- Condescension

Acting From These States Generates Career-Limiting Actions and Behaviors

"You talk over other people."

It's probably obvious that arrogance and overconfidence are not desirable traits in any realm, work or personal. But if you hold on to Belief #8, your mode of operating is based on these undesirable stances. Those around you suffer the consequences.

- You talk over other people.
- You are rude to others who are not as technically competent.
- You withhold information; and, in doing so, you block others from understanding.
- You behave arrogantly.
- You use voice tones and body language that convey the impression that you are demeaning or talking down to others.
- You rattle off acronyms and terms that only someone with your knowledge would understand.

Real World Example: Arrogance = Negative Outcomes

Jim loves technology. He is a mechanical engineer and he develops computer programs that simulate the effects of stress on specific structures. When he talks to non-technical people, Jim assumes he is talking to other engineers from his specific discipline or department. He uses acronyms that only his technical colleagues would know, and he talks rapidly.

This communication approach produces a great deal of frustration in his non-technical colleagues. They have difficulty keeping up with him and understanding what he is saying. But most importantly, when they ask Jim for his opinion in order to help them make a decision, they find it difficult to understand the implications of his opinion.

During conversations, Jim assumes everyone has the same knowledge that he does. But this is not the case. Instead, he comes across as disinterested, arrogant, insensitive, and elitist, making communication difficult and strained. This is especially true when non-technical people, such as those from the legal department or sales, ask questions for clarification.

His manager values Jim's technical competence, but Jim's career is being held back because he cannot effectively communicate with people outside of his department. His next promotion would be to a management position that would require that Jim be influential across departmental boundaries. Jim's manager is not yet convinced that Jim understands what it means to be able to communicate and influence across departments. She has placed Jim's career on hold until he masters this next competency. See Figure 16.1.

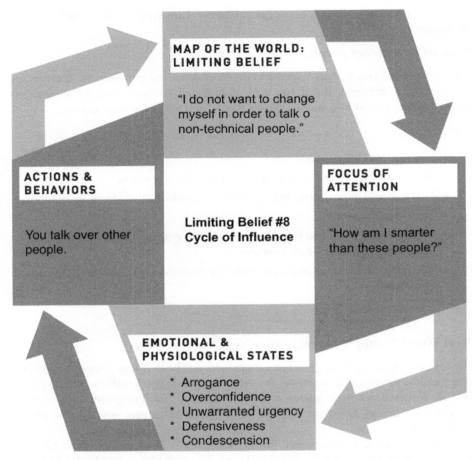

FIGURE 16.1. Career-Limiting Belief #8 Cycle of Influence.

Add Gem of Wisdom #8 to Your Current Map of the World

I must translate technical information: "I understand that it is my responsibility to help others to understand me. I cannot expect everyone to become technologically savvy. I must translate and communicate information in an appropriate manner so that others can understand me."

As a professional coach, when I conduct my workshops I often ask people, "Who is responsible for effective communication? Is it the sender, the receiver, or both?"

Some people select "both" as their answer. Many people have been taught that it takes two people (or all parties) to have a clear communication. Some people select the recipient as their answer. Likewise, many have been taught that good listening skills are important, and so they respond that the listener is responsible for understanding.

My answer is that the *sender* has the *primary responsibility* for effective communication because the sender is the only one who knows what the desired message really is. Therefore, you must—as the engineer, the technical manager, the technologist—send a message that can be decoded properly by your recipients. It is your task, as the subject matter expert, (and the subject matter is your message, whatever that is) to ensure proper reception. It is up to you to cross the bridge to your audience's level of understanding. It is up to you, the one who knows the real intent of the message, to ensure that the listener receives the message as you intended.

Adding Gem #8 Properly Realigns Your Focus of Attention

"How do I connect with my audience?"

Adding this Gem of Wisdom, which is really just the ability to step beyond your own technical mindset and take responsibility for being understood, will shift your Focus of Attention in very positive ways. Instead of looking for where your audience might be ignorant, you will find yourself looking for areas where you can expand their understanding:

- Where are they misunderstanding me?
- How much does my audience understand what I have said?
- How can I best frame my information for my audience?
- How is the communication progressing?
- Does my audience really understand what I am saying and what are the implications? If they do not understand, how do I fix the situation?

Gem #8 Leads to More Useful Physiological and Emotional States

The shift in perspective will generate new emotional and physiological states that can lead you toward greater communication and understanding. Some of those positive states are:

- Openness
- Curiosity
- Confidence
- Concern for others and their work
- Vulnerability

Gem #8 Can Lead to Career-Enhancing Actions and Behaviors

Learn to communicate through a question-and-answer process to ensure that your message is being received as intended. In this way, you can communicate effectively with anyone in almost any situation.

Communicating effectively is something that can be learned. You probably feel you communicate well with your friends. Do you communicate with them well because they are your friends, or are they your friends because you communicate well with them? Whatever your answer, the skill of communicating well does not have to be available only when you talk with your friends. In my workshop titled "Influencing Without Authority for Technical Professionals," I teach how to communicate with anyone in the same way you communicate with your friends, with the same results.

Effective communication is best described as a step-by-step process structured as a feedback loop. Certain steps are necessary to ensure excellent communication. If you learn and deploy these steps, you can influence people in ways that will make you the envy of your organization. By adding this Gem of Wisdom to your professional repertoire, you will move past negative behaviors. In fact, some of the new behaviors that can be expected will make you a desirable employee and colleague.

1. **You will use non-verbal and verbal communication cues to connect with your audience, just as you do when communicating with your friends.**

2. **You will ask questions to determine two things: (a) how your audience wants to receive your message, and (b) how well your audience is receiving your message.**

3. **You will adjust your message to align it with the way your audience best receives and understands your message.**

Let's take a look at each of these actions and behaviors in more detail.

1. **You will use non-verbal and verbal communication cues to connect with your audience, just as you do when communicating with your friends.** Communication happens on several levels at once, not just with the words we speak. The use of verbal and non-verbal communication cues will allow you to powerfully connect with other people so you can convey your ideas clearly, accurately, and effectively. This process of connection is the first step toward achieving powerful and elegant influence.

2. **You will ask questions to determine two things: (a) how your audience wants to receive your message, and (b) how well your audience is receiving your message.** There is little utility in assuming that your audience understands your message without verifying that assumption. It is much better to know exactly how your message is being received, and the only way to determine success is to ask questions. The questions you ask can be very direct, as long as it is clear that you are asking for clarification so that you can be more effective in your communication. The answers you get back from your audience should guide you in your next step of communication.

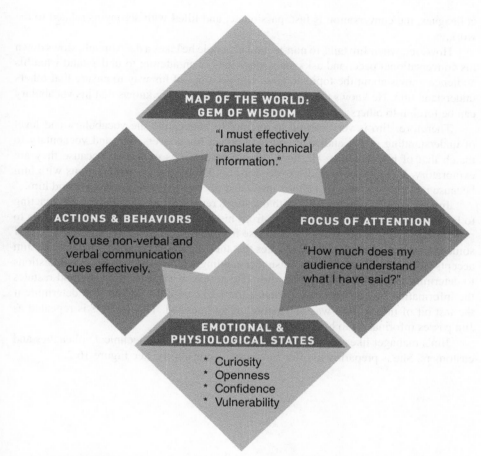

FIGURE 16.2. Career-Enhancing Gem of Wisdom #8 Cycle of Influence.

3. **You will adjust your message to align it with the way your audience best receives and understands your message**. Effective communicators have one trait in common: they are very willing to be flexible in their communication process, ensuring that their message is received as intended. Your willingness to be flexible in your communication style will directly affect your ability to influence others. You must be willing to adjust your message so it can be easily understood by your audience.

Real World Example: Gem of Wisdom #8 in Action

Jim loves technology. He is a mechanical engineer and he develops computer programs that simulate the effects of stress on specific structures. When he talks to his departmental colleagues, the conversation is fast, passionate, and filled with acronyms related to the work.

However, when Jim talks to non-technical people he takes a deep breath, slows down his conversational pace, and asks many questions in an attempt to understand what his audience knows about the topic at hand. Jim goes out of his way to ensure that others understand him. He knows that his perspective is unique. He knows that his vocabulary can be foreign to others.

Therefore, Jim is very careful to attempt to understand the vocabulary and level of understanding of his audience and then adjust his conversation and vocabulary to match that of his audience. He finds these conversations enjoyable because they are exploratory. It is a process of discovery for him. People enjoy conversations with him because it is clear to them that Jim is interested in ensuring that they understand him.

Jim peppers his conversation with questions regarding how his audience is reacting to his information. When the response from his audience is positive, Jim continues to provide information. But when the response from his audience is one of confusion, or if someone makes a statement that indicates that they did not understand what he said, Jim accepts full responsibility for the misunderstanding. He backtracks and asks questions to determine where his audience lost him. He notices what was confusing and restates the information in a different way. Then Jim checks with his audience to determine if the last bit of information was understood as he intended. This process is repeated as Jim passes information to his non-specialist audience.

Jim's manager likes the way Jim communicates with non-technical colleagues and customers. She is preparing to offer Jim more responsibility. See Figure 16.2.

17

Limited Visionary: Career-Limiting Belief #9

"I do not have to think systemically. I am paid only to do my task."

Engineers are trained to do a job, but some have shortsightedness when thinking about how their individual tasks contribute to the whole enterprise. They think, "Someone else will figure out how my work fits into the overall scheme of things." It does not work that way. It is important for engineers, technologists, and technical managers to think outside their immediate world. It is imperative to think beyond your isolated bubble and to begin thinking systemically.

If Career-Limiting Belief #9 Is Part of Your Map of the World...

"All I need do is focus on my own work. My colleagues can just do their own work."

I am constantly coaching engineers and other technical professionals who behave as if their tasks are the only tasks of importance. They act as if whatever decisions they make will not affect anyone else. They ignore the impacts of their decisions on others. *Nearly*

The Fully Integrated Engineer: Combining Technical Ability and Leadership Prowess, First Edition. Steven T. Cerri.
© 2016 The Institute of Electrical and Electronics Engineers, Inc. Published 2016 by John Wiley & Sons, Inc.

every decision you make will, in some way, affect other people, other tasks, and other departments.

Therefore, it is important to understand that your work must be coordinated with the work of others who might be affected by whatever you do. You must think *systemically*, which is having the essential skill of being curious about and becoming aware of how what you are doing can affect other departments, people, and projects.

Career-Limiting Belief #9 Produces a Narrow Focus of Attention

"My reward comes from doing a good job on my tasks which, therefore, shrinks my organizational responsibility and impact."

When you are not thinking systemically and you are only thinking about your own task, you restrict your perspective. Some of the questions or thoughts you might put your attention on as a result of this limited vantage point might sound like this:

- My reward comes from doing a good job on my task. I'll do my job well.
- I do not care what other people are doing; that is their responsibility.
- My boss will tell me who or what to think about beyond my task.
- Thinking about how my task fits with others is what management does.
- I am paid to do my job. I am not paid to be concerned if others are doing their job.

Career-Limiting Belief #9 Results in Undesirable Physiological and Emotional States

The ill-advised Focus of Attention list above will bring on certain specific, emotional and physiological responses in you. Some of the generated states that can be expected are these:

- A false sense of independence
- Arrogance
- An overdeveloped sense of or need for privacy
- Aloofness
- Control
- An overdeveloped sense of ownership
- Defensiveness

Limited Visionary Generates Career-Limiting Actions and Behaviors

"I do not ask others how their tasks are moving along."

Ultimately, your Map of the World and your Focus of Attention engender negative emotional and physiological states, prompting actions that are not in your best interest. Some of the actions that clearly represent Limiting Belief #9 might look like these:

- You do not ask others how their tasks are moving along.
- You only tell your boss about your own tasks and not how your work might impact others.
- You do not ask how your task fits into the larger project.
- You make decisions as if they only affect your task and you do not take into account the potential for the farther-reaching effects of your decisions.

Real World Example: No vision = Negative Outcomes

George has been the procurement manager for a calculator manufacturing company for a little over a year. He has six employees on his team and his department is responsible for the procurement of all parts for the company.

George's manager has incentivized him to reduce the costs of raw materials, which means that George and his team are not focused on overall calculator life cycle cost, only the cost of the raw materials (i.e., before the calculators are assembled). For this reason, George is constantly looking for ways to reduce any possible material costs.

However, the incentive process has an unintended consequence; it drives George to avoid thinking systemically. He does not really care much about how anything he does affects other departments. As long as he can procure workable parts at a reduced cost, then he is doing his job well, and George and his team will receive their bonuses.

The calculators are made of plastic and are assembled with metal screws. George has found a new vendor for the screws, and each piece will cost a few cents less; this adds up to a significant amount over the span of a year. The savings will translate into a bonus for George and his team at the end of the year. Through a verbal discussion with the vendor and a text description of the screw, he orders thousands of the new screws.

The new screws arrive, and within minutes of the screws arriving on the calculator assembly line, the calculator manufacturing process comes to a halt. It seems that the screws are manufactured with a small flange at the end. It is part of the screw manufacturing process, not part of the screw specification. Therefore, the vendor did not call out to the procurement manager that the flange existed.

However, because of the flange, the metal screws bottom-out in the plastic calculator screw hole and strip the plastic threads. The calculators cannot be assembled using the new screws. Before the old screws can be re-ordered and received at the assembly line, three days of calculator manufacturing shut down occur. George has brought the whole calculator assembly line to a halt for three days because he did not think systemically. See Figure 17.1.

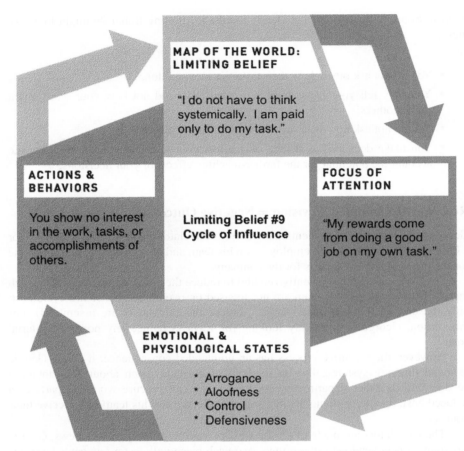

FIGURE 17.1. Career-Limiting Belief #9 Cycle of Influence.

Add Gem of Wisdom #9 to Your Current Map of the World

Think systemically and see the bigger picture: "I understand that my organization exists in a system. The success of the system depends on each component working in concert."

Successful people understand that they must look beyond their immediate organization. They understand that they must help coordinate every part of the organization that they impact and touch. They also know that they do not work in isolation.

Adding Gem #9 Brings Out a New Perspective in Your Focus of Attention

"Who needs to know what I am doing?"

Adding this Gem to your Map of the World will shift your Focus of Attention, positively. It allows for more expansive perspectives to form, taking root from questions such as these:

- Who might be surprised by what I am doing?
- Who needs to know what I am doing?
- What do I want to know about what others are doing?
- How is my work going to fit into the bigger picture?

Gem #9 Prompts More Useful Physiological and Emotional States

The shift of Focus of Attention will, in turn, generate new emotional and physiological states. Some are listed below:

- Openness
- Curiosity
- Vulnerability
- Confidence

Gem #9 Can Produce Career-Enhancing Actions and Behaviors

"I will talk to anyone who may be impacted by my work."

You must begin to understand that you do not function in a vacuum. Your tasks are part of a group of tasks that must be integrated. Thinking in this way will lead you to find connections between what you and your colleagues are doing. It is important to find the cause-and-effect relationships of your actions beyond your immediate areas of involvement.

By adding the Gem of Wisdom #9 to your Map of the World, you will see yourself acting anew.

1. **You will mentally picture how your work can have impact, both inside and outside your organization.**
2. **You will seek out others in an attempt to understand what they do and how your work might affect them.**
3. **You will keep your manager and others informed of your work in order to engage in a discussion about possible impacts.**

Let's delve into more detail and see how these behaviors might show up in an organizational setting.

1. **You will mentally picture how your work can have impact, both inside and outside your organization.** When you perform a task, do you ever think about how your task might affect other people or other departments? By adopting

systemic thinking you will naturally ask yourself questions about how what you are doing will affect others. In this way, you will be imagining the potential impacts of your work. Whether you are a manager or an individual contributor, adopting this mindset is not only critical to the success of you and your organization, it also makes you a valuable asset to the whole system within which you work.

2. **You will seek out others in an attempt to understand what they do and how your work might affect them.** Some engineers and technologists do not think systemically, so someone has to take the first step. If you adopt this mindset, you will proactively seek out others in order to understand what they do and how what they do affects the project and the organization. You may look a little nosy at first, but if you attempt to understand how everyone's work fits into a larger perspective, you will be seen not as nosy but as someone who can help everyone be successful.

3. **You will keep your manager and others informed of your work in order to engage in a discussion about possible impacts.** Managers cannot be everywhere and cannot know everything. They are dependent upon communication with a wide variety of sources in order to understand if those who report to them are completing their work as expected. If you become someone who can communicate effectively with management and who can keep management apprised of the systemic implications of all of the moving pieces, you will become invaluable to your organization.

Real World Example: Gem of Wisdom #9 in Action

George has been the procurement manager for a calculator manufacturing company for a little over a year. He has six employees on his team and his department is responsible for the procurement of all parts for the company.

George's manager has incentivized him to reduce the costs of raw materials. Specifically, George and his team are not incentivized to reduce overall calculator life-cycle cost, only the cost of the calculator raw materials (i.e., before the calculators are assembled). For this reason, George is constantly looking for ways to reduce any possible materials costs.

But George knows that while his personal incentive program might be to reduce raw-material costs, he understands that his real products are calculators, not the parts of the calculators. He does not work merely to procure parts. He works to build calculators.

The calculators are made of plastic and are assembled with metal screws. George has found a new vendor for the screws. He can procure these new screws for a few cents less per screw and this adds up to a significant amount over the span of a year. The money he will save on the aggregate number of screws will provide George and his team with a very nice bonus by the end of the year.

However, before ordering the new screws, George decides to think systemically. He knows that his actions can affect the production of the calculators on the assembly line. So he orders some sample screws just to be certain that they will work as well or better than the current screws.

He consults with and alerts the manager of manufacturing that some new screws need to be tested and that several calculators should be set aside for the test. The test calculators are pulled off the manufacturing line before assembly. The new screws are used to assemble the test calculators and they fail because the screws are manufactured with a small flange at the end. It is part of the screw manufacturing process and therefore, it is not part of the specification. However, because of the flange, the metal screws bottom-out in the plastic calculator screw hole and strip the plastic threads. The calculators cannot be assembled using the new screws. George decides to continue manufacturing with the previous screws and resumes discussions with the new vendor to determine if there is a fix.

Because George decided to think systemically, he avoided an assembly line shutdown. He asked some questions: How might my decision affect others? How might my decision to procure the new screws affect the assembly line process? Who needs to test these new screws before I procure them as standard parts?" Because George asked these questions, he decided to test the new screws. It was the right decision. See Figure 17.2.

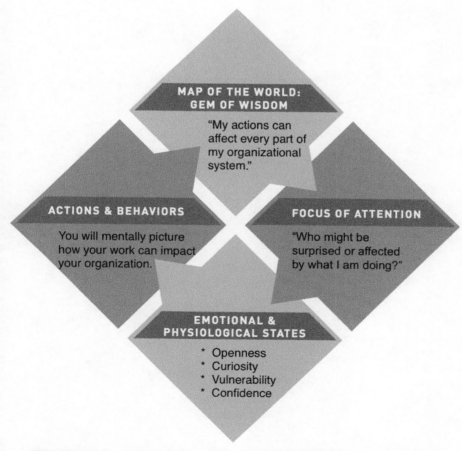

FIGURE 17.2.   Career-Enhancing Gem of Wisdom #9 Cycle of Influence.

18

Being Persistently Consistent: Career-Limiting Belief #10

"What got me here will get me there."

Most engineers, technical managers, and technologists, believe that their past successes are the steps upon which future successes will be built. They believe that what has worked up until now will also work in the future. I can guarantee you that such thinking will not generate a long-term, successful career. Whether you want to remain technically focused or you want to transition to management or any other career path, you must understand that what made you successful at your current level will not make you successful at your next level. Your current success may only be the key to entry to the next level; thereafter, it may be necessary for you to acquire and apply new skills and behaviors.

If Career-Limiting Belief #10 Is Part of Your Map of the World…

"I will just do what I have been doing and I will be successful."

Most engineers believe that what makes them successful at one level of their career will make them successful at the next level and beyond. It is human nature to focus on what works and to keep doing it. Therefore, most engineers do, indeed, believe that what makes them successful in one position will make them successful in the next position.

This misperception is often also held by technical managers who promote engineers to lead positions based on the following thought process: "If that engineer can do her technical work so well, then she can obviously manage a team doing the same kind of work." Seems to make sense, right? But in most cases, it is simply not true.

Transitioning from engineer or technologist to leader or manager is not always smooth, and the new set of responsibilities requires a new way of thinking that probably was not taught to you in college and that seldom comes naturally. For most engineers, the new way of thinking, the new way of being necessary for success as a manager or even as a lead, is often best thought of as a whole new career. It will ultimately require a new identity, a new set of beliefs, and a new set of behaviors. The transition from the technical world to one less technical, like management, or technical sales, or technical lead, or program manager can be thought of as a transition from the certainty of engineering and technology to the ambiguity of human interaction and management.

Remember that human behaviors are driven by emotional states and emotional states are structured by our beliefs and our concepts about the world we live in. If you have spent your career focusing on the structure and certainty of the world of technology (understanding the unambiguous world of the laws of physics, statics, dynamics, fluids, thermodynamics, motion, or structures), then moving into a world where you are charged with leading humans, with all of the unpredictable elements of human interaction and the ambiguity of management, will be like moving to another planet. This transition must be planned for and executed well or it can lead to missteps and delays and perhaps even career-halting failures.

Career-Limiting Belief #10 Creates a Poor Focus of Attention

"I will keep doing what I have always done. It seems to work."

When you believe that the abilities and mindsets that helped you achieve your current successes are necessary for your future successes, then your Focus of Attention will be as follows:

- I know what I am doing.
- I have done this before, and I can do it again.
- This is the way I did it before.
- This looks familiar.
- Where are the similarities between the past, present, and future?

Such Focus of Attention Results in Unhelpful Physiological and Emotional States

The Focus of Attention statements listed above will lead to certain emotional and physiological responses in you that are not desired or useful. Some of the generated states that can be expected are these:

- Inflexibility
- Stubbornness

- Confidence in the predictability of the future
- Unwillingness to accept new ideas
- Unwarranted sense of certainty

You Will Then Enact Ineffective, Stagnant Behaviors

Ultimately, these undesirable elements in your Map of the World and your Focus of Attention generate actions that will impede your success. Some of the actions that clearly represent Limiting Belief #10 are as follows:

- You keep repeating past behaviors even when they are no longer successful.
- You use behaviors that seem out of place for the situation.
- You seem to be behaving stubbornly.
- You find change difficult.

Real World Example: Stagnation and Inflexibility = Negative Outcomes

Betty has been a detail-oriented, technically competent engineer. She has progressed from an entry-level engineer to a senior engineer on the merits of her technical capability and her attention to detail. She has been an individual contributor and she has done well.

Six months ago, she was promoted to a team lead in charge of six people working on a project. She devotes all of her time to managing these six people and the project. She is no longer responsible for individually performing any technical work; her current role is 100% management.

However, she is finding that this new position does not seem to be working out very well. Several of her team members are frustrated, and she is frustrated, too. She is not encouraged by the progress of the team or the project. At the same time, she is doing everything she did in the past to be successful. She is helping the team with its technical issues, focusing on every detail. She is telling her team members how to do their work, noticing when they miss something. She is behaving as a part of the technical team of individual contributors.

Meetings of the whole team happen daily to discuss what technical issues are on the table. She attempts to help each member individually, by showing each person what to do, not hesitating to point out their error and what they must do to correct it.

Despite paying attention to all the technical, programmatic, and management details, the project does not seem to be going well. While she does not know it consciously, Betty is convinced that "what got me here will get me there." She believes that the behaviors that made her successful as an individual contributor—the behaviors that made her successful as an engineer—will make her successful as a manager of engineers. She is not ready to stop being a good engineer, and no one has told her how to behave differently nor has management provided her with appropriate training for her new role. See Figure 18.1.

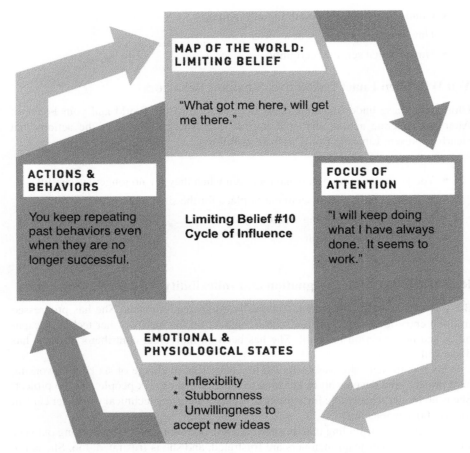

MAP OF THE WORLD: LIMITING BELIEF

"What got me here, will get me there."

ACTIONS & BEHAVIORS

You keep repeating past behaviors even when they are no longer successful.

Limiting Belief #10 Cycle of Influence

FOCUS OF ATTENTION

"I will keep doing what I have always done. It seems to work."

EMOTIONAL & PHYSIOLOGICAL STATES

* Inflexibility
* Stubbornness
* Unwillingness to accept new ideas

FIGURE 18.1. Career-Limiting Belief #10 Cycle of Influence.

Add Gem of Wisdom #10 to Your Current Map of the World

Embracing growth: "I understand that the process of learning does not stop when I begin my work career. In fact, when I begin my work career, I am actually embarking on a new career–a career I never really intended to have or prepared for."

When most engineers first begin working in an organization right out of school, they believe that they are prepared for the work that is to be given to them. And, generally speaking, they are. However, a college degree in engineering usually only prepares people to perform the technical work. Too often, school does not prepare people to do the teamwork or perform the interpersonal communications required for career success.

As you move toward managerial work, or toward advanced individual contributor work, be prepared to learn a whole new way of moving through the world, because your organization wants more than your technical expertise; you need to fit into the organization at a higher level.

Gem of Wisdom #10 Triggers Positive Change in Your Focus of Attention

"What new skills will make me successful?"

Adding this secret to your map will shift your Focus of Attention, prompting your ability to reconfigure your perspective at work.

* What are successful leaders doing that I am not?
* Who can provide me with great advice?
* What do I need to learn?
* What is working?
* What is not working?
* What is missing in my knowledge base?
* Who can help me see my blind spots?
* Do I really want to be a leader or do I just want to do my technical work?

Gem #10 Generates Good Physiological and Emotional States

The shift of focus will, in turn, generate new emotional and physiological states that may be uncomfortable at first, but you will understand that they are necessary and you will become used to them. Some are listed below:

* Curiosity
* Comfort with uncertainty
* Comfort with unpredictability
* Comfort in being operationally flexible

Gem #10 Will Lead You Toward Career-Enhancing Actions and Behaviors

"I will learn to be open to what is required for success at my new level. I assume that I need new tools in my toolbox. I will become a sponge for learning about the successful tools and behaviors modeled by positive leaders around me."

Over the course of your life, your technical career will take many twists and turns. What may have begun as an engineering career may end up…well, who knows where?

Your flexibility and your willingness to adapt will determine your long-term success, and that success will be in direct proportion to your ability to learn, change, grow, adapt, morph, and leave behind inadequate old habits while adopting new ones that will increase your odds of success.

Most people will not have the careers they anticipated, expected, wanted, or trained for. Those people who attain and retain precisely the jobs they went to school for are the exceptions. You will be a rare bird if you train to be an engineer and you are an engineer when you retire. This does not mean you cannot have the career you originally intended, I just mean that you will have to consciously work to maintain it.

While career change may be the one constant, it also will be important for you to understand the root source of your personal happiness—the core identity that gives meaning to your life—and to use that as the primary weight that grounds you while, at the same time, modifying your behaviors to be successful in the new challenges you will face. This balancing act, between necessary flexibility brought about by new career opportunities and your sense of personal identity and happiness, provide the path to career success and personal happiness long-term. By adding the Gem of Wisdom #10 to your Map of the World, you will generate new behaviors such as these that can help you be successful:

1. **You will look at the behaviors of people around you who are successful.**

2. **You will be open to the suggestions of others, including your manager, regarding new behaviors that will allow you to be successful.**

3. **You will seek out a mentor who can help you navigate within your organization and along your career path.**

Let's delve into more detail regarding these actions and see how they might show up in an organizational context.

1. **You will look at the behaviors of people around you who are successful.** Behaviors have consequences. Certain behaviors are more or less successful in certain contexts. Therefore, it is important for you to notice what success looks like at various levels in your organization. Pay attention to who is successful at different levels of your organization, analyzing what attitudes and behaviors contribute to their success.

2. **You will be open to the suggestions of others, including your manager, regarding new behaviors that will allow you to be successful.** Invariably, you will hear people tell you what you need to do to be successful. Much of the time you will not hear them or the information will not sink in. It is important that you listen to the advice of those who are successful if you want to advance. They are showing you the path. If you like where they are pointing you, then heed their advice.

3. **You will seek a mentor who can help you navigate within your organization and along your career path.** If you can, find a person you like, respect, trust,

and is senior to you and who likes and respects you. Then ask that person to be your mentor. Virtually anyone who ultimately achieves high levels of success has had one or more mentors along the way. You should, too.

Real World Example: Gem of Wisdom #10 in Action

Betty has been a detail-oriented, technically competent engineer. She has progressed from an entry-level engineer to a senior engineer on the merits of her technical capability and her attention to detail. She has been an individual contributor and she has done well.

Six months ago, she was promoted to a team lead in charge of six people working on a project. She devotes all of her time to managing these six people and the project. She is no longer responsible for individually performing any technical work; her current role is 100% management.

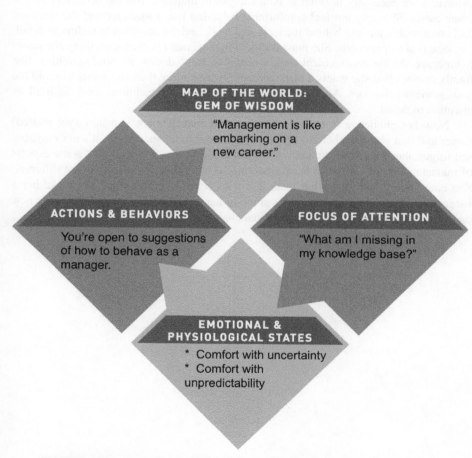

FIGURE 18.2. Career-Enhancing Gem of Wisdom #10 Cycle of Influence.

However, she is finding that this new position does not seem to be working out very well. Several of her team members are frustrated. Betty is also frustrated, and she is not encouraged by the progress of the team or the project.

She is doing everything she did in the past to be successful, helping the team with its technical issues and focusing on every detail possible. She is telling her team members how to do their work, noticing when they miss something. She meets with all team members daily to discuss what technical issues are on the table, attempting to help them personally by showing them what to do.

Betty finally realizes that she has not changed her behavior since she became a manager. She now understands that she has been acting like a technical member of the team, which now she is not. She has been acting as if what made her successful as an engineer will make her successful as a manager. She realizes she was behaving as if she was still a part of the team rather than behaving as their manager.

A change is needed, so she enrolls in management training classes to learn what behaviors are necessary in order to be a successful manager. But the behaviors do not come easily. She does not feel comfortable behaving like a manager and she does not feel comfortable leaving behind the technical work and the attention to technical detail.

She is at a crossroads. She must decide if management is even something she wants to embrace. As the management classes progress, Betty does some soul searching. She finally decides that she wants a management position more than she wants to avoid the management behaviors. And she is willing to give up her technical work with all its attention to detail.

Now her challenge is in understanding that management is a new (yet related) career and that she must behave differently in order to be successful. It's not easy, but she forges ahead because she knows it is what she wants. She finds that some aspects of management are similar to her past technical work, but many aspects are different. She now understands that what made her a successful engineer will not make her a successful manager. As she abandons some of her old behaviors and adopts some new ones, she embarks on a process of personal change. See Figure 18.2.

19

Pursuing Perfection: Career-Limiting Belief #11

"It is important to make my product, task, or deliverable perfect."

Most engineers that I have worked with have an unconscious belief that their product, task, or deliverable can always be made better. Just a little more work here, a little more attention there, a little more detail on this part and the product will be perfect. Many engineers do not understand when their product or task is sufficiently complete for them to stop working on it. The key is to understand when "enough is enough." You will never be able to stay within budget, complete a task on time, or manage others if you do not understand how to evaluate when a task is satisfactorily complete instead of perfect.

If Career-Limiting Belief #11 Is in Your Map of the World...

"Everything I do must be perfect."

Too many engineers believe that because they are being evaluated on their individual work, they must ensure that the product they deliver is perfect or very nearly so. It is common for engineers to not quite (at any point in the process) be ready to release their software, or deliver their analysis, or hand off their report.

This tendency to strive for perfection is drilled into us in our college years. It is coupled to the belief that your engineering work is a reflection of your identity (remember Career-Limiting Belief #1) and to the belief that you must be right (recall Career-Limiting Belief #2).

In college, while delivering the right answer is important, there is often "extra credit" for that extra effort. We carry that unconscious association between extra effort and reward into our work environment. Once inside an organization, we can quickly acquire the reputation of not being willing to let go of our deliverable. We gain the reputation of never quite being finished. We hear ourselves saying things like, "It is almost done," Or "I just need a little more time to finish it," or "If I had a little more time, I could make it really great."

Our Map of the World is filled with beliefs around the idea that perfection is desirable and that it is something that can be achieved. The reality, however, is that it cannot be achieved. The truly successful engineer, technical manager, or technologist knows how to evaluate a task or project to determine when a project has met its goals.

Career-Limiting Belief #11 leads to an Ineffective Focus of Attention

"I need to make this perfect."

When you believe that perfection can be achieved and that it is the only path to success, then your Focus of Attention will be as follows:

- I know I can make this better.
- I just need a little more time to make it just right.
- They do not really understand what this task should look like; I will deliver this product perfectly and show them what good work I can do.
- I know how to make this perfect.

Such a Perspective Moves You to Negative Physiological and Emotional States

The Focus of Attention statements listed above will lead you down a path that isn't productive. You will be motivated by the following emotional and physiological states:

- Stubbornness
- Combativeness
- An overdeveloped sense of ownership
- Feelings of needing more

Career-Limiting Belief #11 Reinforces Undesirable Actions and Behaviors

"I will not release my work until it is absolutely perfect."

Ultimately, it all adds up to actions and behaviors that will limit your success at work and elsewhere. Your need for perfection, beyond what is expected, leads to these types of actions:

- You display excessive ownership of a task or product.
- You show an unwillingness to release a deliverable when others are satisfied with it.
- There is unwillingness, on your part, to adhere to a schedule or budget.
- Delivery dates are rarely made.
- In meetings, you say things like, "It will take as long as it takes."

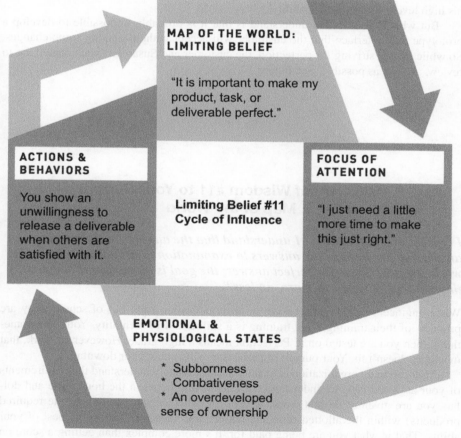

MAP OF THE WORLD: LIMITING BELIEF

"It is important to make my product, task, or deliverable perfect."

ACTIONS & BEHAVIORS

You show an unwillingness to release a deliverable when others are satisfied with it.

Limiting Belief #11 Cycle of Influence

FOCUS OF ATTENTION

"I just need a little more time to make this just right."

EMOTIONAL & PHYSIOLOGICAL STATES

* Subbornness
* Combativeness
* An overdeveloped sense of ownership

FIGURE 19.1. Career-Limiting Belief #11 Cycle of Influence.

Real World Example: Pursuing Perfection = Negative Outcomes

Pete is a programmer and he has been assigned to deliver a software package. The task, schedule and budget are divided into two major phases. Phase A is a rapid prototype process, and he is tasked to deliver a prototype user interface for customer review and approval. Phase A is scheduled to last six months, and Phase B is to last twelve months. Phase B is the development of the signed-off prototype into a fully functional, working interface.

Pete is three months into Phase A. His manager, Susan, is anxious because she had expected that the customer would have reviewed Pete's work by now. However, Pete does not want to release his prototype. He claims it is not ready yet. Both Susan and the customer are concerned, but Pete keeps saying that he needs more time, and the holdup is not well articulated.

In his work, Pete is actually attempting to develop the prototype interface without a flaw before he gives it to the customer for review. For that first review, he wants the customer to say, "It is just perfect." He feels that a perfect first demo will demonstrate his high level of technical capability.

But what Pete does not understand is that it is probably impossible to develop a prototype user interface that the customer will accept without making some changes. So while Pete is striving for perfection, the customer and Susan just want something to review, as soon as possible. See Figure 19.1.

Add Gem of Wisdom #11 to Your Current Map of the World

Progress over perfection: "I understand that the answers to the problem I am solving are not like the answers to examination questions in college. At work, the goal is not the perfect answer; the goal is an answer that meets the required criteria. No more, no less."

When engineers first begin working in an organization right out of school, they are products of their training. That training is a skill-and-drill mentality. You learn something; then you are tested on it. Perfection means a high grade. However, at work, that mentality doesn't fit. Your pursuit of perfection will lead to your downfall.

Your job in an organization is to fully and completely understand the requirements of your assigned task, to understand the relationship between the hours/time and dollars you are given to do that work, to estimate whether you can deliver the required product(s) within the allotted time and budget, and then to do so to the best of your ability. That is what you are being paid for. It's more complex than getting a score on a test.

Adding Gem of Wisdom #11 Shifts Your Focus of Attention, Allowing for Growth

"I need to truly understand what is expected of me."

Adding this secret to your Map will shift your Focus of Attention, allowing you to re-assess your own old work patterns. You will then be able to develop new ways of working toward a satisfying end.

- What are my task requirements?
- How much time have I been given?
- What is my budget?
- Does the task, the budget, and the time allotted all make sense?
- Can I do this? Who can help me?
- What are the risks to my success?
- Do I truly understand what the deliverable is?
- Have I completed the task as set out in the requirements?

You Will Enable Positive Physiological and Emotional States

When you begin to ask the right questions regarding your work habits, your mindset will shift. In this case, you will begin to see how finding the "sweet spot" in your task's completion is beneficial for the whole team. You will notice a change, and so will your coworkers. Your behaviors will be driven by the following emotional and physiological states:

- Curiosity about what is enough or too much
- Shared ownership for projects
- Analytical perspectives that move work toward completion
- A desire for communication that moves projects forward and uncovers the true project status
- A heightened task awareness

Gem #11 Triggers Positive Actions and Behaviors

"If I truly understand my role as an engineer in my organization, my career will skyrocket. This does not mean that I do not push the envelope at times; I will and I do. It does not mean that I do not do more than is asked at times; I will and I do. But attempting to deliver a perfect product is no longer a programmed reaction for me."

As an engineer, being able to assess and deliver what is expected and no less or no more is the beginning; you will now develop the sense of judgment and perspective that is the foundation of good individual contribution. It is also the foundation of good management and leadership.

The pertinent question for your advancement to management is this: "How can you be expected to manage the work of other people, keep their tasks within requirements, within budget, and on schedule, if you cannot keep your own tasks within these parameters?" Of course, the answer is "You cannot."

Similarly, managers must understand what is needed for the delivery of a completed project or product, and they must be able to communicate these requirements to others.

Therefore, your ability to advance to management and then to succeed at management significantly depends on your ability to manage yourself.

Some of the behaviors that might appear as a result of adding Gem of Wisdom #11 to your Map of the World are these:

1. **When assigned a task, you will ask questions that clarify acceptable deliverable conditions.**

2. **You will evaluate that task in relation to the time, money, and other resources needed to complete the task.**

3. **You will proactively communicate the status of the task or project without being asked to do so.**

Let's look in more detail at these behaviors in the real world.

1. **When assigned a task, you will ask questions that clarify acceptable deliverable conditions.** Much of the time, when an engineer or technologist is given a task, many assumptions are made by both the manager and the engineer. The manager wants to empower the employee, perhaps by not giving the employee too much detail. The manager will often give just enough information to define the deliverable without indicating the process of developing or completing the required deliverable. The employee, not wanting to look incompetent, will hesitate, failing to ask all the possible questions that could lead to a complete understanding of what the task requires. And so both retreat to their respective offices, blissfully unaware that they are on a collision course with failure.

   If you truly want to be successful as a manager or an individual contributor, it is important to ask clarifying questions that will eschew false assumptions. Anything less than a complete understanding of what is expected will result in the mismatch between actual task completion and the unattainable ideal of task perfection.

2. **You will evaluate the task in relation to the time, money, and other resources needed to complete the task.** Very often, a project task comes with a completion schedule. Invariably, the employee accepts the task description, hours, and completion schedule without much evaluation as to the accuracy of those boundaries. But it is important for that employee, the person actually doing the work, to evaluate whether the task can actually be completed in the hours and schedule allotted. Without such an up-front evaluation, it is often the case that the allotted hours and time can run out before the task is completed to satisfaction.

Before accepting a task, an employee should, if possible based on prior knowledge and experience, evaluate whether the task, hours, and time allotted all make sense.

3. **You will proactively communicate the status of the task or project without being asked to do so.** When employees seek perfection, they are not interested in stopping work to tell others how their task is progressing. They bury themselves in their work and focus on doing everything to make the project perfect.

If you really want to control your need for perfection, take the time to stop what you are doing and give a status update to your manager. Take this opportunity to discuss, honestly, how the task is moving forward, noting advancements or roadblocks equally. This discussion ought to help you see where you might be focusing more on perfection as opposed to the actual requirements. Remember, your long-term career is not dependent on perfection but on getting the job done.

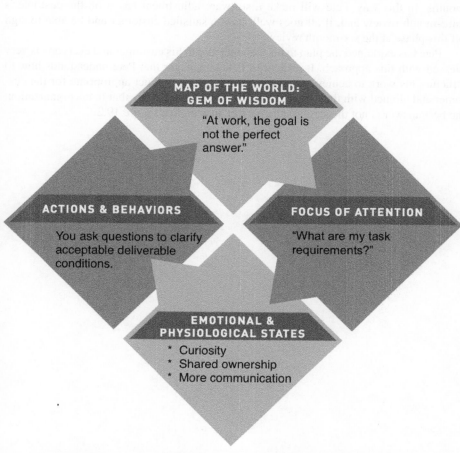

MAP OF THE WORLD:
GEM OF WISDOM

"At work, the goal is not the perfect answer."

ACTIONS & BEHAVIORS

You ask questions to clarify acceptable deliverable conditions.

FOCUS OF ATTENTION

"What are my task requirements?"

EMOTIONAL &
PHYSIOLOGICAL STATES

* Curiosity
* Shared ownership
* More communication

FIGURE 19.2.   Career-Enhancing Gem of Wisdom #11 Cycle of Influence.

Real World Example: Gem of Wisdom #11 in Action

Pete is a programmer and he has been assigned to deliver a software package. The task, schedule and budget are divided into two major phases. Phase A is a rapid prototype process where Pete is tasked to deliver a prototype user interface that the customer is to review and hopefully, provide approval. Phase A is to last six months and Phase B is to last twelve months. Phase B is the development of the signed-off prototype into a fully functional, working interface.

Pete is three months into Phase A, and he is ready to release his first pass at the prototype interface. He understands the true purpose of his work. He is not there to produce the "best, most awesome interface possible" all on his own. He understands that the final decision-maker as to the appropriateness of the interface is his customer.

Therefore, Pete understands that the more input he has from his customer, the more his interface will meet the customer's expectations. He has decided that he will provide his customer with two interface preview sessions: one at three months and one at six months. In this way, Pete will make a software adjustment based on the customer's third-month review and, if all goes well, have a satisfied customer and be able to sign off this phase at the six-month review.

Pete has explained the plan to his manager and to his customer and everyone is very pleased with this approach. It is clear to Pete's manager that Pete understands how to structure his work to achieve the desired outcome—a product appropriate for the customer and aligned with the task requirements. Pete understands that in his organization, the best answer is not the same as the perfect answer. See Figure 19.2.

20

You are Not the Teacher: Career-Limiting Belief #12

"Non-specialists need to know everything I know."

Many engineers, technical managers, and technologists believe that if non-specialists want to understand a technical concept, then they need to know every small detail. As someone who has been technically trained, you often consider your ability to convey details to be an advantage to your ability to convince, influence, and persuade others, especially non-technical people. A more effective approach is to understand your audience and give them just what they need in order to come to the necessary and appropriate conclusion.

If Career-Limiting Belief #12 Is Part of Your Map of the World

Many engineers and technologists are enamored with their discipline. For them, engineering and science are the foundations for making sense of the world. Along with this belief is the corollary that everyone else needs the same level of technical prowess in order to make sense of the world. They believe that if they are going to explain something to others, especially those that do not have technical training, it is imperative that they (the audience) should understand every little detail. Those engineers often fall into the trap of sounding like they are giving a "class-room lecture" on the technical matter.

The Fully Integrated Engineer: Combining Technical Ability and Leadership Prowess, First Edition. Steven T. Cerri.
© 2016 The Institute of Electrical and Electronics Engineers, Inc. Published 2016 by John Wiley & Sons, Inc.

We have all seen it. A non-technical person asks a question, and a simple, non-technical answer will do just fine. However, the engineer begins at the beginning, defining parameters, setting up structures, and outlining constraints. Then, using technical terms, answers the non-technical person's question in a way that only a technical person would appreciate.

The non-technical person still does not have a satisfactory answer but is so confused or frustrated that it is impossible to formulate a follow-up question. The engineer is satisfied that the question has been answered because the non-technical person has not responded. This scenario plays out constantly in our technical world. But a better approach is available. It requires that engineers, technologists, and technical managers understand three important facets of this scenario.

First: Your goal is to provide information so that non-technical people can understand and make informed decisions. That is called *influence* and it is always the purpose of any conversation.

Second: In order to influence others, the influencing must take place in the mind and the perceptions of the *listeners*, not in the mind of the speaker.

Third: You must, therefore, understand what non-technical people need in order to make informed and appropriate decisions. Your ability to influence relies on your ability to get out of your own thought patterns and to engage with what the listeners need.

In order to successfully complete these steps, you must begin by asking questions. That is, if someone who does not have your specific technical prowess asks you (the technical person) a question, be sure to ask questions to ascertain the level of knowledge and the breadth of informational gaps before providing an answer. Based on the answers received, you can then provide answers that are appropriate to both the level of technical knowledge and information held by your audience.

As well, there is no need to give more information than what is necessary for your audience. There is very little advantage in burdening non-experts with the minutiae, unless absolutely necessary (rare, indeed). Start at their level of knowledge and then build from there, providing information as needed or requested.

In a nutshell, answering questions from non-technical people is best done after a series of questions (from the technical person) that determines the level of technical knowledge of the audience and then begin there to inform them as appropriate to their needs.

Career-Limiting Belief #12 Generates a Misaligned Focus of Attention

"Let me tell you what you should know."

When you believe that everyone should know the same highly specialized information that you know, then your Focus of Attention allows you to ignore others, to your own peril. Not realizing the specific needs of others in your work lets you think thoughts like these:

- Let me tell you what you should know.
- That is not the right question to ask me.
- It is clear you do not know what you need to know.

- I am really smart and you should just trust me; you should understand what I already know.
- I ought to explain this to you (in great detail).

These Thoughts Create Ineffective Physiological and Emotional States

Those Focus of Attention statements listed above are powerful, and they will produce certain specific, emotional and physiological states. When such negative and damaging perspectives enter your thought process, they allow you to believe that you are better than others. The states you might experience are:

- Arrogance
- A desire for detail and specificity
- A desire to elaborate
- A false or misplaced sense of ownership

You Will Then Enact Career-Limiting Actions and Behaviors

Ultimately, this misaligned Map of the World, along with your predictable Focus of Attention, generate emotional and physiological states that are, generally, undesirable for work situations. Career-Limiting Belief #12 leads a person to these kinds of poor behaviors:

- You begin to talk as if you are teaching a class…a class no one signed up for.
- You will pontificate.
- You ignore the non-verbal cues from non-technical listeners that indicate that you have lost their attention and/or their understanding.
- You continue talking well after the audience's attention has waivered.
- Your manager interrupts you to move the conversation along.

Real World Example: Detail Overkill = Negative Outcomes

Susan is a good engineer, and when she talks about technical topics, her enthusiasm is evident. However, Susan's enthusiasm is so strong that she often ignores what her audience really wants to know. She answers questions as if she has to explain everything. It has been said of Susan, "Ask Susan what time it is, and she will tell you how to make a watch." Often when non-technical people ask Susan a question, she seems to answer a completely different question.

Susan and her manager, David, are in a meeting with two members from a company that is a potential customer. Participants in the meeting from the other company include the manager and the lead project engineer. This meeting is important to Susan's company because, if the customer truly understands the benefits of the proposed product, the sale could mean large revenues for her company.

The potential client's manager has asked Susan a question that warrants a relatively simple answer. But instead of addressing the answer to the manager, Susan answers the question as if the engineer asked it. And while the engineer is eager to hear her explanation, the manager's eyes glaze over. Susan has lost him. Of course, Susan and the engineer are on the same wavelength, and they are engaged in an animated conversation. Both Susan's manager and the potential client's manager are watching the conversation go on, completely sidelined.

When she is done with her overly-technical explanation, the manager looks at his engineer for clarification. He only says "Yeh, that's right."

This exchange has not made the potential client's manager happy. Susan's manager David, sensing that the meeting is falling apart, asks Susan to restate answer for him, keeping it to a level he can understand. It's an astute move on his part, as David is asking for clarification for himself, rather than embarrassing his potential clients. The answer she gives this time allows everyone to understand.

All is well, but only because Susan's manager stepped in to help clarify the answer. However, this is not a good day for Susan. Her manager has now decided that Susan cannot be left alone in a room with a non-technical customer without someone there to manage Susan's communication process. It is clear that Susan is incapable of talking to a non-technical audience. See Figure 20.1.

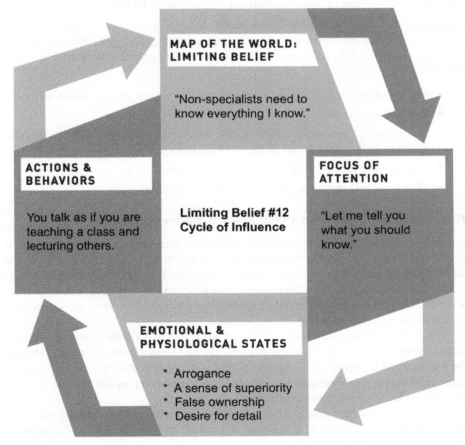

FIGURE 20.1. Career Limiting Belief #12 Cycle of Influence.

Add Gem of Wisdom #12 to Your Current Map of the World

Be effective: "I am more effective when I provide audience-appropriate information."

Engineers are unique. Like people trained in any highly specialized discipline, engineers have a high level of topic-specific knowledge. Most people do not need such deep engineering/technical abilities to do their work. Engineers must realize that it is not incumbent upon them to transform the non-technical person into a technical expert.

The key stumbling block for many engineers is that they often assume that there is a fundamental minimum amount of information and understanding that everyone must have in order to comprehend a topic or to come to a sound, reasoned conclusion. Engineers mistakenly believe that the minimum level of information and understanding needed to make a decision is not based on the person making the decision; but rather, they choose to believe that the decision will be made solely on the engineer's concept of "truth." This belief lets over-zealous engineers evangelize a bit on technical issues, not understanding that the engineering details are not required (many times) for others to make decisions. This approach triggers a predictable process that, in most cases, results in more information than is necessary and asked for by others. (Note: Enthusiasm is not the same as evangelizing. You can always be enthusiastic; enthusiasm is good…just answer the question put forth.)

A better approach is one in which the engineer starts with "What do I need to bring to the table so that others can make an informed, reasoned decision from their perspective?"

In this way, when communicating with non-technical people, the engineer, technologist, or technical manager must be sensitive to different audiences and their level of technical prowess. The more you can take these factors into account, the more successful you will be in communicating, influencing, and convincing people of your position.

Adding Gem of Wisdom #12 Allows for an Expansive Shift to Your Focus of Attention

"What does my audience need to know?"

Adding this Gem of Wisdom to your Map will shift your Focus of Attention to the following:

- What is the question I am being asked?
- What questions will help me understand this person's current level of knowledge?
- What does this person already know?

- What are the important gaps in her/his knowledge and understanding?
- What information can I provide that will help this person make an informed and reasoned decision?

Gem of Wisdom #12 Will Pave the Way Toward Positive Physiological and Emotional States

The shift of focus will, in turn, generate new emotional and physiologically states. Some are listed below:

- Curiosity
- Sensitivity
- Openness
- Hesitation

Gem of Wisdom #12 Allows for Career-Enhancing Actions and Behaviors

"I will learn that I am not just a source of knowledge and information. I can help others to become competent enough to make their own informed decisions."

This process is extremely important to your long-term career success. As you move forward, you will become more involved with people who are not engineering or technical experts. They are from other fields (such as business, law, accounting, leadership, efficiency assessment, safety assuredness, governmental oversight, environmental control) and you need to be part of that team.

Therefore, your ability to communicate with them in a way that makes sense to all will become more and more critical. Your ability to seem like a congenial and supportive educator rather than a pontificating hot-air machine will make a huge difference in your ability to navigate the professional hurdles that invariably appear as your career matures.

Knowledge and information do not stand alone. All information needs context in order to provide meaning. Therefore, technical data cannot be the only structure that allows people to make informed and reasoned decisions; you must provide the context as well as the information. Keep in mind that the unique challenge here is that the *context resides in the mind of the person making the decision.* If someone asks you a question and you answer it without considering context, you will probably miss the mark, since your answer will only make sense to you. Doing so will probably mean that your communication will not be in context for the other person. Your answer may have little or no meaning for your audience.

Putting this process into practice means that you must take into account the context of the person asking the question, providing a targeted answer. The only way to do this is to ask enough questions beforehand in order to frame your information in way that makes sense for the receiver.

By adding the Gem of Wisdom #12 to your Map of the World, you will generate new behaviors such as these:

1. **You will ask questions of your audience in order to understand what they know and do not know; in this way, you will receive a clearer understanding of what they are really asking.**
2. **You will tailor your answer to align with their knowledge.**
3. **You will continually adjust your communication in order to create a fully-realized context for everyone concerned.**

Let's look at each of these actions and behaviors in more detail to determine how they might appear in the general work context.

1. **You will ask questions of your audience in order to understand what they know and do not know; in this way, you will receive a clearer understanding of what they are really asking.** When you answer a question without assessing your audience, by default, you answer the question as if you are talking to yourself. The other possibility is that you may just be guessing what the other person knows and does not know, attempting to fill in the gaps. Either of those approaches is weak, at best. It is much better to know your audience authentically, rather than to guess. There is only one way to find out this information with any certainty: you must ask questions before you give your answer.

   In my workshops, I have a reputation for not answering a question from a participant without first asking several questions. The reason I do this is that I have no idea how much the participant knows. Before I move to answering the question I think they are asking, I want to find out if my assumptions are correct. Once I ascertain what they know, I am better equipped to truly answer their question.

2. **You will tailor your answer to align with their knowledge.** Once you understand the audience's knowledge level, you can tailor your answer, attempting to provide information in a useful way and at an appropriate level. This process will make you so much more effective when answering questions from both technical and non-technical people.

3. **You will continually adjust your communication in order to create a fully-realized context for everyone concerned.** As you become more adept at asking questions for this purpose, you will find that this is a continuous process that allows you to learn, too. You will realize that you ask a question to receive clarification. You then answer in an appropriate way. Your audience may ask you another question, or you may ask a follow-up question to your answer in order to determine how your answer "landed" in the other person's brain.

This back-and-forth process continues as you refine the Question and Answer process so that your audience gets exactly what is needed, allowing for a fully-informed decision. Once you get good at this process, you will become the go-to person for people who want to understand difficult and complex concepts.

Real World Example: Gem of Wisdom #12 in Action

Susan is a good engineer, and when she talks about technical topics, her enthusiasm is evident. Susan's enthusiasm is so strong that she sometimes ignores what her audience really wants to know and can really comprehend. She answers questions as if she has to explain everything. It has been said of her, "Ask Susan what time it is, and she will tell you how to make a watch." Often when non-technical people ask Susan a question, she seems to answer a completely different question.

However, Susan has recently learned a new technique of asking clarifying questions before she answers the questions posed to her. It's an unfamiliar process to her, and it seems a little odd. For years, she thought she was supposed to just answer the question. After all, she is the expert, isn't she?

But she has been practicing this process and it seems to work well. Whenever she is asked a question, unless she is absolutely certain of the level of knowledge of the audience, she will not answer outright.

Instead, she will respond with a query of her own…or perhaps several! She poses questions that are designed to gather more information about the other person's needs. By asking good questions and listening hard, she really understands what the person is asking. This questioning process has proved very useful.

Susan has an important meeting scheduled and she is anxious to see how this approach works. Susan and her manager, David, are in a meeting with two members from a company that is a potential customer. These clients include the manager and the engineer. This meeting is important to the company because if the customer truly understands the benefits of the proposed product, the sale could mean large revenues.

The customer-manager has asked Susan a question that warrants a relatively simple answer. Susan takes a deep breath and asks him a question designed to clarify how much he already knows about the technology. His response shows that he does not really know that much about the technology. Susan asks another question in order to determine if he even understands the implications his original question.

His response clearly indicates that he is asking a question that does not really bear upon the decision he wants to make. Out of respect, Susan wants to answer his question, but she needs to do so in a way that provides context, allowing him to be fully aware of the outcomes.

Susan now begins to guide him by giving him a little knowledge that shows him that he may be asking a question that is not very useful. She indicates a better question by connecting a new question to the decision he apparently wants to make. He understands the connection and eagerly changes his question to be more aligned with the technical information that he will need to have to make a sound decision.

She answers his new question in a clear, simple fashion and he then asks another question. This back and forth continues for a couple of minutes and it becomes clear that

FIGURE 20.2. Career-Enhancing Gem of Wisdom #12 Cycle of Influence.

the customer-manager is fully understanding. He clearly likes what Susan is telling him, and he clearly likes the proposed product. It is a good conversation and meeting. Susan's company gets the contract. David is pleased, and he is now less likely to accompany Susan to customer meetings. Susan has clearly shown that she can effectively communicate with both technical and non-technical people. See Figure 20.2.

21

Withholding Expertise:
Career-Limiting Belief #13

"It is wise to withhold information in order to maintain control and influence."

As the educational system sets up learning, student engineers become conditioned to believe that their success is tied to their own knowledge and contribution. As a result, they ultimately begin to believe that they are in competition with other engineers on the team. This may be a hidden belief, not easily seen. But they begin to think that their intelligence and contribution are measured against the intelligence and contribution of those around them, as if in a competition. Often, this leads them to withhold important information, believing that doing so allows them to maintain control, influence, and job security.

If Career-Limiting Belief #13 Is Part of Your
Map of the World....

"Withholding and controlling information allows me to seem important."

Because the typical engineer's education process teaches that student's grades are directly related to intelligence and contribution, many engineers join organizations with a mindset that they are in competition with their colleagues.

The Fully Integrated Engineer: Combining Technical Ability and Leadership Prowess, First Edition. Steven T. Cerri.
© 2016 The Institute of Electrical and Electronics Engineers, Inc. Published 2016 by John Wiley & Sons, Inc.

Indeed, many organizations foster this sense of competition. Your performance reviews are based on your own contribution. And many aspects of our work environments teach, in subtle and not so subtle ways, that even though you are expected to work on a team, you are also evaluated on your individual abilities as they stand in comparison with others. Some employers seek to promote subtle and low-level competition, while other organizations foster outright competitive environments that allow yelling, screaming, and other overt forms of competitiveness.

While most people function reasonably well in the more subtle competitive environments, every now and then, an engineer decides that in order to survive on the job, he or she must play the competitive game a little more covertly. This often shows up as a set of behaviors we can group under the label of "withholding information in order to maintain control, influence, and job security."

People who display this type of behavior have decided that it is in their best interest to look like an expert to others. They believe (and it may be true) that they are subject matter experts (SMEs), and they know more than others do. The negative impact comes when they internalize a mindset where they cannot let information out into the open without first ensuring that people are ready for it or worthy of it.

This behavior pattern is usually generated from a position of fear—a fear that their position is at risk or that they will not be valued enough. From this perspective, they do everything they can to build up their perceived value to the organization, which often takes the form of "I am the expert, and the organization just cannot afford to lose me."

Career-Limiting Belief #13 Produces an Ineffective Focus of Attention

"I have information that others do not."

When you believe that you are at risk and you must ensure that others know how valuable you are, then your Focus of Attention will be as follows:

- How can I show that I know more than they do?
- Where are others wrong?
- Where can I correct what others have said or written?
- What information can I hide that will make me look important?
- How do I ensure that I am the only in-house expert on this subject?

This Focus of Attention Generates Negative Physiological and Emotional States

If the questions above form a strong part of your day, the resulting mindset is unproductive and even harmful to your stature inside your organization. Some of the specific emotional and physiological states generated might be:

- A feeling of arrogance
- A feeling of fear
- A feeling of aggression toward the expertise of others

Career-Limiting Belief #13 Encourages Pontification

Ultimately, all of those poor beliefs, mindsets, and states affect how you act at work.

- You talk as if you are lecturing.
- You are prone to pontification.
- You "talk down" to people.
- You wait for people to make a mistake and then you pounce on their error.
- You do not like to have meetings in which you are forced to divulge what you now.
- You hesitate attending meetings unless you can control them.

Real World Example: Withholding Expertise = Negative Outcomes

Pete is a senior engineer. He has been elevated, over the years, to a status of unofficial "internal consultant," which is a position that crept up on Pete. It did not happen overnight; it was a slow gradual process.

He now behaves like a consultant much of the time and many of his colleagues are generally dissatisfied with him. Most people do not like working with Pete because he withholds information (despite the "consultant" demeanor), comes across with an arrogant attitude, and generally only reluctantly provides answers when needed. And when he does provide answers, they are at the very last minute. This behavior has annoyed many of his colleagues, but they need Pete because he seems to have information and answers that no one else has.

Recently, the company has received a résumé from an engineer who is half Pete's age and who could come on board as an employee at a much lower salary. Also, this new candidate seems to have the interpersonal people skills that Pete lacks.

Pete's management has evaluated and compared Pete's salary, benefits, and retirement package costs to those associated with the potential new hire. As well, management considers the "aggravation costs" Pete brings to the table with each project. While Pete has valuable on-the-job experience and some significant company history, that combination does not seem to outweigh the problems that Pete causes by withholding important information during projects. Also, with the possibility of the purchase of new software, the younger, less experienced engineer can solve many, but not all, of the technical problems that Pete used to solve. Therefore, after taking into account all these factors, company management has decided that it is time for Pete to go. They have decided to use a typical reorganization process to ease Pete out.

However, before proposing the new reorganization, management had decided that it is necessary to capture Pete's knowledge in order to help the younger engineer come up to speed in the new position. This will happen by enticing Pete to develop and teach several in-house courses on his considerable expertise.

Pete is flattered that he has the opportunity to showcase his knowledge and teach others what he knows. He believes that this is also an opportunity to show how valuable he is.

Once Pete has created the course materials and presented them several times, management decides to put the reorganization into place, announcing its implementation; Pete's position will not exist in the new organizational structure. A new position will be established with new job requirements, specifically designed to keep Pete from successfully applying. A new position for Pete cannot be found within the company, and so Pete is laid off.

The newly created position was specifically designed to allow the new hire to successfully apply. However, everyone knows that the new position is just Pete's old job in new clothes. Unlike Pete, the new hire is someone who is willing to cooperate and be a team player with management.

Everyone enjoys working with the new hire. She is smart, seems to have many (though not all) of the answers Pete had, plus she enjoys sharing what she knows. Everyone is happy and no one in the organization misses Pete. See Figure 21.1.

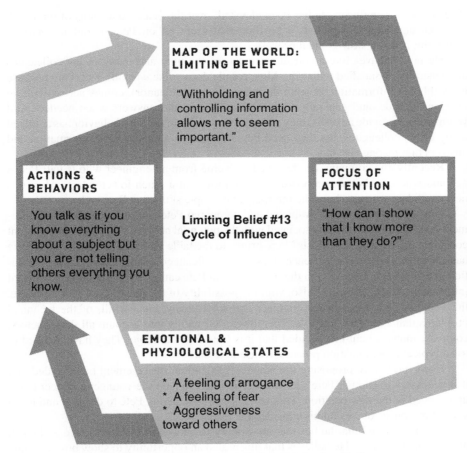

FIGURE 21.1. Career-Limiting Belief #13 Cycle of Influence.

Add Gem of Wisdom #13 to Your Current Map of the World

Generosity with knowledge: "I understand that sharing what I know makes me more valuable. I must continue to learn in order to not make myself obsolete, but the goal is to be a learning machine that brings new information to everyone. That makes me invaluable."

When you take an examination in college, your answers are supposed to be your own. You are not allowed to discuss your answers with the person next to you. However, in an organization when you are part of a team, competing with your colleagues is not productive. Shared answers are, indeed, the desired outcomes.

Now I know there are some organizations where competition between colleagues is the norm. Companies like Amazon®, Apple®, Intel®, and Oracle®, just to name a few, have reputations for internal competition and battles that are legend. However, even in such competitive environments, these tactics are nothing more than a different way to produce a shared answer or outcome. So while there may be those who would disagree with me, my philosophy is that if you are on a team, then be part of the team and contribute what you know. I would argue that withholding information does not serve you or the team or the organization or the project. It is destructive to everyone, and, ultimately, to your career.

To be sure, it takes personal confidence to give away information that, were it closely controlled, would make you appear indispensable. However, having the confidence to share expertise can do more for your career than withholding information to maintain a false sense of power.

Adding Gem #13 Opens Ways for Your Focus of Attention to Allow for Growth."

"How can I contribute?"

Adding this secret to your Map will shift your Focus of Attention to the following:

- What information can I provide that will make this project progress smoothly?
- What information do people not know that they do not even know to ask?
- What information can I provide that will show that I can contribute expert advice in this area?
- How can I contribute to the whole team's success?

Gem #13 Brings Productive Physiological and Emotional States

The shift of focus will, in turn, generate new emotional and physiological states. Some are listed below:

- Openness
- Desire to participate
- Contribution
- Curiosity

Using Gem #13 Allows for Positive Actions and Behaviors

"I will learn to be open with what I know. Sharing information will make me more valuable–not less."

If you adopt this approach, you will surely become much more proactive, productive, and valuable. You will be seen as a source of important information, and you also will be seen as someone who is willing to share that information readily.

People will be more willing to come to you for advice because you will be seen as welcoming. They will feel comfortable making requests of you. This, in turn, will make you easily accessible for professional information, making you more valuable.

The process continues and you become a critical, necessary, and important part of the success of the organization. Now you are a valuable SME in the organization—not because you hold on to information but because you freely share it.

Some of the behaviors that you will exhibit are:

1. **You are a sponge for new knowledge and information.**
2. **You know how to integrate new information you acquire into the company's critical path to provide the highest Return on Investment (ROI).**
3. **You seek to understand as much as possible about what different programs and projects need and you proactively seek to share what you know.**

Let's take a closer look at these behaviors in an organizational context.

1. **You are a sponge for new knowledge and information.** This behavior is, in most cases, typical of engineers and technologists. Constant learning is a critical component of your career success. However, constant learning is also critical to the accomplishment of behavior #2 below.

2. **You know how to integrate new information you acquire into the company's critical path to provide the highest Return on Investment (ROI).** Acquiring and holding information may increase your perceived importance, but it does not necessarily advance an organization toward its goals. The information and knowledge you have is useless unless it is applied, and how and to what end it is applied are equally important. It is important for you to find the critical paths,

those outcomes that are most important to your organization or your company. Next it is critical to determine the tasks that advance that outcome and that provide the most "bang-for-the buck." This is, as a minimum, where you should focus your efforts.

3. **You seek to understand as much as possible about what different programs and projects need and you proactively seek to share what you know.** While you might want to wait for people to come to you with a problem, don't. Go seek out problems that you can help solve. Being proactive in sharing knowledge is better than being reactive.

Real World Example: Gem of Wisdom #13 in Action

Pete is a senior engineer. He has been elevated, over the years, to a status of unofficial "internal consultant." The unofficial status of internal consultant crept up on Pete. It did not happen overnight; it was a slow, gradual process.

When Pete began to behave like a consultant, and when he began to behave as if he was the only one who had specific knowledge, his colleagues were generally dissatisfied with him. They let him know of their dissatisfaction, and Pete picked up on their non-verbal, negative behaviors as well.

It became clear to Pete that most people did not like working with him. He was not being treated with the respect that he thought he was supposed to receive as a major SME.

He had one or two really close colleagues and one day Pete mustered all his courage and went to each of them separately and asked for advice. He told them that he thought people did not like working with him anymore and he wanted to know what had changed.

He was told, in no uncertain terms, that withholding information and playing "power trips" with his knowledge was not only hurting the team but it was probably going to hurt his career. He was delaying providing his answers until the last minute and he was attempting to make the others on the team seem less knowledgeable.

Pete got the message. He became a source of specific, technical knowledge. He became a help, rather than a hindrance, in providing people with information, even creating an online library for the company. However, his particular brand of sage advice was still needed for certain projects. This combination has made a major difference in his career success. Pete understood that he had to accomplish several things in order to be successful as his company's unofficial internal consultant.

First, he had to be constantly learning more and more about his subject. If he was going to be a source of expert information, he had to be continually updating that expertise.

Second, he wanted to be regarded by others as an expanding source of that information. Therefore, he had to do something that consistently informed his colleagues and the organization that Pete was a reliable expert in specific areas. And this requirement led him to the third step.

Third, he had to share that information so that people understood his value to the organization. Pete decided to share information through lunch-hour lectures at his company, written papers, published internally as well as published externally in journals, and even at field-specific conferences.

As he began to implement these three steps, his credibility rose. The tensions between Pete and his colleagues disappeared, and he became a more valued expert in the organization.

Pete's company is constantly receiving résumés from young and very qualified engineers who are applying for jobs. But Pete's position is never on the chopping block.

Now, Pete is truly a valuable asset to the company. His technical knowledge coupled with his real-world experience, plus his company-specific knowledge and experience, make him a one-of-a-kind contributor. This is exactly where Pete wanted to be. See Figure 21.2.

Note: When I first graduated from college and began my aerospace career, I met several SMEs at Rockwell International, the builder of the Apollo and Shuttle spacecraft. These

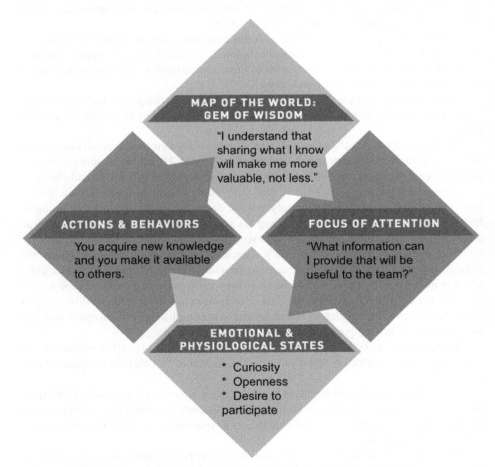

FIGURE 21.2. Career-Enhancing Gem of Wisdom #13 Cycle of Influence.

senior internal consultants were highly valued by the company and when I went to them with questions they were extremely helpful and forthcoming with information. I speak about people like Pete not as an idea or an aspiration, but as real people. I have met people like Pete, who have the Gem of Wisdom in their Map of the World, at many different companies. They exist and have been very helpful in my career and in the careers of others. Will you become a Pete in your organization?

22

Bluntness as a Virtue: Career-Limiting Belief #14

"Being blunt is being honest, and being honest is being accurate with data."

Facts are facts. Data are data. Most engineers, technical managers, and technologists have spent much of their time dealing with the seemingly black-and-white world of data, information, equations, and technology. They have avoided the often messy, human interaction that is filled with ambiguity, emotion, and the constraints of real life. So is it any wonder that many technical people come across as blunt, arrogant, and rude? It is time to change that.

If Career-Limiting Belief #14 Is Part of Your Map of the World...

"I can just tell it like it is."

Most engineers have spent their time working with the black-and-white world of technology: $F = ma$; $E = IR$; the laws of thermodynamics; Newton's Laws of Motion; and software that either works or not. These laws and models do not bend depending upon blood sugar levels, or mood, or what has happened during the morning commute.

The Fully Integrated Engineer: Combining Technical Ability and Leadership Prowess, First Edition. Steven T. Cerri.
© 2016 The Institute of Electrical and Electronics Engineers, Inc. Published 2016 by John Wiley & Sons, Inc.

These laws and models are consistent. Dependable. Predictable. They do not vary with emotion. They cannot be argued with.

After years of working with such rock-solid tools, is it any wonder that many engineers, technical managers, and technologists move through the world as if everyone also is an engineer…or should be?

If all we have is a hammer, everything looks like a nail.

If all we have dealt with in the past are the physical laws of the universe, everything we deal with now looks like a reflection of those laws.

Therefore, engineers begin to deal with their human counterparts as if they, too, understand that everything is simply the result of the laws of the universe. I think for many engineers and technologists, thoughts like the following rant can often go through our heads:

Why bother with this thing called human sensitivity? Human sensitivity is not real. There are no physical laws describing it. It varies continually, depending upon whom we are dealing with, what happened to them during their morning commute, and how they are feeling at the present moment. These parameters and conditions are purely arbitrary and transitive. They mean nothing and will go away in a short while anyway. So let's just deal with the facts. And, by the way, let me explain what the facts are…

As an engineer, scientist, technical manager, and ultimately general manager, I can tell you that these thoughts never really go away. When you have embarked on a career in which your main goal is to understand how the physical laws of the universe work, it is easy to forget that the majority of the world is centered on the human condition. Interestingly, much of what we do as engineers is to try to improve the human condition.

Our human counterparts do not behave as unambiguously and as consistently as Newton's Laws of Motion, nor do we. As a human, you are often driven by emotions just like everyone else. If you think that you are always logical, that you behave like a Vulcan (remember Spock of *Star Trek*?), I would disagree. Even when you believe you are making logical decisions, I can reasonably argue that emotion plays an important part. (Note: being insistent that you are only logical is an emotional response in and of itself) And when you become upset because someone is challenging your ideas or your data, it is emotion that you feel.

So even though you may think that you are a logical machine, that you make your decisions by weighing hard facts, it just is not true. You emotions play a significant role in your life, both professionally and personally.

Therefore, if you want to be successful in the world of people, you must begin to understand that being blunt, stating the facts, and just working with facts will not necessarily get you to the results you want.

Career-Limiting Belief #14 Ensures Ineffective Focus of Attention

"I just care about the facts."

When you believe that verifiable information is the only important element in decision-making, and that we can be blunt with that information and refuse to contextualize it, then your Focus of Attention will likely reflect shortsighted positions like these:

- What are the facts?
- When can I tell you the facts?
- I just want to tell you something so you will understand.
- I know that you do you not know what you are talking about; let me set you straight.
- The facts and data should be the only factors in decision-making.

These Stances Put Ineffective Physiological and Emotional States into Play

The Focus of Attention statements listed above will produce certain specific, emotional and physiological responses in you that allow for some misaligned perspectives. The emotional and physiological states you may experience include:

- Feelings of impatience
- Feelings of wanting to be inflexible
- Lack of consideration
- A feeling of arrogance
- Over-certainty about your ideas

You Then Enact Career-Limiting Actions and Behaviors

Ultimately, your Map of the World and your Focus of Attention generate emotional and physiological states that can lead to some of the following undesirable behaviors.

- You speak louder than is necessary.
- You talk over other people.
- You speak in a condescending manner to others.
- You demean the information provided by others.
- If people do not agree with you, you discount their information.

Real World Example: Bluntness = Negative Outcomes

George is the consummate engineer. His speech is precise. His logic is impeccable. He speaks less from feelings and more from the perspective of data. But he seems to be constantly arguing because he finds weak points in the reasoning of others and pounces on those weak points. He constantly corrects people.

From George's perspective, he is just speaking the truth. He does not buy into the theory that anyone should have to sugarcoat his/her statements. He is not calling the other person stupid or ignorant, nor does he yell. All he is doing is stating fact…after fact…after fact…after fact.

From George's perspective, the facts are self-evident. For others, George's so-called facts are not so obvious. When George interacts with colleagues and customers, he is seen as rude, arrogant, and a know-it-all. This is especially true when George interacts with colleagues and customers from other cultures. Some cultures are much more sensitive to blunt behavior than his US colleagues. Some of his international colleagues have complained to management about his behavior. He is very close to being laid off because most people do not want to work with him.

George's manager has brought in a coach to help George through this process. If George cannot figure out how to correct this rude behavior, he may not have a job next year. See Figure 22.1.

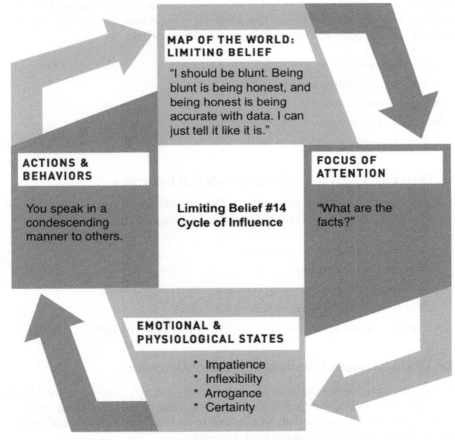

FIGURE 22.1. Career-Limiting Belief #14 Cycle of Influence.

Add Gem of Wisdom #14 to Your Current Map of the World

Fine-tune the channel: "I understand that influence and effective communication are composed of two pieces: the data and the communication channel that the data travels on. I realize that I must cultivate relationships so that the communication channels are open before sending my important message."

Think of communication as a carrier wave on which you are sending a message as a signal. The message, the signal, is superimposed on the carrier wave. The carrier wave is specific and ensures that the receiver will receive the message at the other end. The message/signal rides along on the carrier wave and is decoded at the receiving end.

The transmitter sends out the message upon the carrier wave to the receiver. The message is superimposed on it. If the receiver operates at the same frequency as the carrier, then the receiver will be able to decode the signal and receive the message. However, if the transmitter frequency is different than the receiver frequency, the transmission will never be received and the message signal will never be decoded.

You can see that it is important for the transmitter carrier wave frequency to be the same as the receiver frequency for the message to be received smoothly. In human terms, the analogy means that the person sending the message must communicate in the same communicative style as that of the audience.

If George is attempting to communicate with another person, George must adjust his communication style to duplicate the preferred communication style of the other person. If George is not willing to adjust his communication style (i.e., the carrier wave of his message) to that of his audience, his communication style can appear to be too different from that of the audience; therefore, communications will shut down and his message will not be received.

Let me restate that last point in a different way: the perception of being rude is not an absolute behavior. There is no absolute measure of rudeness. In a very real sense, rudeness is merely a large variation between the way the sender is sending the message and the way the receiver would like that message to be sent.

Rudeness is merely the representation of a large gap between the sender's preferred communication style and the receiver's preferred communication style. When that gap reaches a certain value, the communication moves from being annoying to being rude. So to avoid being perceived as being rude, offensive, and/or too blunt, adjust your communication style to that of your audience; the effectiveness of your communication will increase exponentially. (This, actually, is a relatively easy process when you know how. For further instruction in this area, please see the referenced bibliography, item [1], [2], and [3]. As well, feel free to contact me, Steven T. Cerri, directly by going to www.stevencerri.com.)

Adding Gem #14 Enables a Positive Shift in Your Focus of Attention

Adding this Gem to your map will shift your Focus of Attention toward a more productive way of interacting with others. You will discover a significant shift in the way you frame your own perspective.

- How can I best convey my message?
- How are they communicating with me?
- How should I best communicate with them?
- How can I make sure what I am saying will make sense to others?
- What is their preferred communication style?
- How should I adjust my communication style to match that of my audience?

Gem #14 Allows for More Productive Physiological and Emotional States

The shift of focus will, in turn, generate new emotional and physiological states in you. Some of the new states will be:

- Curiosity
- Calmness
- Flexibility
- Helpfulness
- Interest
- Patience

Adding Gem of Wisdom #14 Means You Demonstrate Career-Enhancing Actions and Behaviors

"I will learn to notice how others communicate with me and I will match their communication style. This will help me avoid being rude or inconsiderate in my communication process."

Many engineers, technical managers, and technologists come across in their communications as rude and inconsiderate. This common behavior seems to be the result of the belief that information and data need to be raw in order to be valid.

This is truly a wrong-headed approach. While the communication between a satellite transmitter and ground receiver is certainly a black-and-white process with no emotion entering into the equation, this is not the case for human beings. People do have emotions, and communication is always…always…a contextualized act, which means that the meaning of a communication is determined by the emotional and physiological states (i.e., their perspective) of the listener. Avoid this truth at your own peril.

Human communication is a process that needs to be considered differently. In communication between people, your primary function is seldom just the transmission of data or the transmission of information. In most situations involving human communication, the desired outcome is some sort of influence or some sort of movement toward a decision that one or more of the parties want. This requires the consideration of human needs and human emotion.

Your goal is to understand that people want more than data when you are communicating with them. They want a connection with the informant, and that connection comes about through alert communication processes.

Some of the behaviors that might be evident when you add the Gem of Wisdom to your map are these:

1. **You adapt your communication style to match that of your audience.**
2. **You ask questions to understand what is important to your audience.**
3. **You are sensitive to how your message is being received by your audience and you adjust your process to achieve your desired meaning in the audience.**

Let's look at how these behaviors might appear in a work context.

1. **You adapt your communication style to match that of your audience.** Being blunt is not always the most effective way to get your ideas across, and being honest does not always require being blunt. The two do not necessarily go hand-in-hand. When you understand that you must adjust your communication style to match that of your audience, you will behave in ways that allow you to connect. This connection to your audience will enable you to send any message in a way that will be heard by your audience, regardless of the intensity, severity, significance, or importance.

2. **You ask questions to understand what is important to your audience.** You have seen this behavior before. Communication and influence rest on the premise that your message must align with the Map of the World of the *listener,* the audience. In order to understand how to frame your message for your audience members, you must understand something about what your audience thinks is important and what they do not. You can only understand what your audience believes is important by asking questions in order to determine what is important to them. Once you understand the importance of understanding the Map of the World of your audience, you will ask questions well before you begin presenting your data. This is especially critical for those of you who work with people from countries other than your own. Not only does each person have a different Map of the World based on personal experiences, each person's map is also filled with cultural and regional biases that are often unknown to those from other cultures or regions. Therefore, questioning your audience is critical. Whether your audience is made up of kindred spirits or nationals from around the world, you can never ask too many respectful, map-revealing questions before you send your important message.

3. **You are sensitive to how your message is being received by your audience and you adjust your process to achieve your desired meaning in the audience.** It is

absolutely critical to understand that in influencing others, your goal is to control the way the message is being received by your audience. You are attempting to control the meaning of your message. Adjusting your communication style to conform to your audience's preferred communication style is key. This may seem like a very difficult process but it is not. For more information on how to accomplish this, please see [1], [2], [3].

Real World Example: Gem of Wisdom #14 in Action

George is the consummate engineer. His speech is precise. His logic is impeccable. He speaks less from feelings and more from the perception that he is data-driven. He seems to be constantly arguing because he finds weak points in the reasoning of others and pounces on those weak points. He constantly corrects people.

From George's perspective, he is just speaking the truth. He does not have to sugarcoat his statements. He is not calling other people "stupid" or "ignorant," nor is he yelling at them. All he is doing is stating fact…after fact…after fact…after fact.

From George's perspective, the facts he puts forth are self-evident. For others, George's so-called facts are not so obvious. This produces a context where George is seen as a rude, arrogant, and a know-it-all. And George is very close to being laid off because no one wants to work with him.

George's manager has brought in a coach to help George through a process of improving his communication. If George cannot figure out how to correct what is seen as rude behavior, he may not have a job next year.

With some soul-searching, George begins to understand that facts alone do not make for effective communication. Effective communication, by definition, is not just the transmittal of data and/or information. It is a combination of being heard and being able to move people in the direction that the communicator wants them to move. This is called *influence* and George knows that being perceived as rude will not lead to influence.

At first George has an aversion to the term "influence." George never considered himself someone who influenced others. As a good engineer, he assumed that his job was to put data on the table, to present the facts and let people come to their own conclusions.

But as George has progressed in his company, it has become clear that his manager, and his company, want George to convince people that certain conclusions are better than others. Just presenting data is not enough. George's job has now become presenting data and pointing the audience toward a specific interpretation of that data. This is influence.

George begins to understand that, as much as he would like it to be different, his ultimate goal therefore, is to influence his audience, and transmitting data without considering how that data is transmitted or how it is received is not sufficient for success. He begins to ask himself, "How do I communicate in order to more effectively influence my audience?"

George begins to learn how to determine, through casual conversation, the desired communication style of his audience. As he learns this, he begins to adjust his communication process to match that of his audience. Slowly, George begins to notice that his communication with others becomes smoother and more effective. His performance

FIGURE 22.2. Career-Enhancing Gem of Wisdom #14 Cycle of Influence.

reviews are better and more positive, and he begins to understand that being effective and influential means that he must be aware of two components of communication: the data and the communication process. Both have become important to George.

George also notices that the preferred communication style of his audience not only changes from person-to-person, but also from one culture to another. Each culture has a generally preferred communication style that is universally preferred by the people in that culture. Within that culture, each individual has a unique preferred communication style, as well. At first all these variations seemed a bit overwhelming to George, but with some practice he notices that he is able to adjust in real time to the preferred communication style needed. He now finds the whole process of communicating with others to be easy, fun, effective, and very respectful. See Figure 22.2.

References

[1] S. Knight, *NLP at Work: The Essence of Excellence, (People Skills for Professionals)*, 3rd ed., London, Nicholas Brealey Publishing, 2009.

[2] G. Claxton, Intelligence in the Flesh, Yale University Press, New Haven and London, 2015.

[3] J. Riggio, *The State of Perfection: Your Hidden Code to Unleashing Personal Mastery*, Smashwords Edition, 2012.

23

The Fixer: Career-Limiting Belief #15

"I should look for what is wrong and what will not work because I am here to fix problems."

Engineers are trained to build things, to solve problems, to find solutions to major challenges. They are conditioned to answer questions. This training predisposes them to move through the world ready to pounce on something—anything—that does not work or must be solved. This predisposition often flies in the face of the personal philosophies of team members who may be looking for possibilities. This juxtaposition of personal perspectives causes problems for many technical professionals.

If Career-Limiting Belief #15 Is Part of Your Map of the World...

"I fix things."

Most engineers believe that they are problem solvers. I have heard many engineers tell me that their job is to find problems and fix them. You have probably been in meetings where some of the people are talking about what can be accomplished and an engineer is telling everyone why "this" cannot work and why "that" will have a problem. You have probably been around engineers who perpetually seem to have their proverbial glass half empty instead of half full.

I have worked with and coached many engineers and even technical managers who seem to go around with a dark cloud over their heads, constantly looking for the problem

---

The Fully Integrated Engineer: Combining Technical Ability and Leadership Prowess, First Edition. Steven T. Cerri.
© 2016 The Institute of Electrical and Electronics Engineers, Inc. Published 2016 by John Wiley & Sons, Inc.

in a situation. While others are looking for the silver lining, these engineers are looking for any potential stumbling block.

It is not difficult to understand where this thinking comes from. In the education of the typical engineering student, the underlying, unspoken message is, "You, the engineer, are in the world to solve problems."

While this may seem an innocuous perspective, it can sometimes translate into a doom and gloom way of looking at the world. Turning over every rock, asking every question, approaching every project from the perspective of "Where are the hidden gremlins?" Ultimately, your colleagues will tire of hearing this perspective.

Career-Limiting Belief #15 Encourages a Gloomy Focus of Attention

"I know there is a problem somewhere."

When you believe that the world is filled with problems that you must discover and solve, then your Focus of Attention will be as follows:

- I know there is a problem somewhere.
- What can go wrong with this situation?
- How do I solve this problem?
- I am worthless if I cannot find a problem to solve.
- My job is to turn over every rock and find the hidden problem.
- Other people seem to have a naïve, overly positive perspective.

Career-Limiting Belief #15 Produces Negative Physiological and Emotional States

The Focus of Attention perspectives listed above will produce certain specific, emotional and physiological responses in you. Some of the generated states that can be expected are these:

- Mistrust
- Uncertainty
- Negativity
- Dissatisfaction

This Generates Career-Limiting Actions and Behaviors

Ultimately, your Map of the World and your Focus of Attention generate emotional and physiological states that generate the impetus for action, and it's probably not action that is in your best interests. Some of the actions that clearly represent Limiting Belief #15 are these:

- You keep looking for what will not work.
- You keep bringing up potential problems to even the simplest of situations.
- You get a reputation of being the harbinger of doom and gloom.
- You tend to disagree with any new idea and challenge others to defend it.

Real World Example: Doom and Gloom = Negative Outcomes

Barbara was a good mechanical engineer. In fact, she had progressed to engineering manager of a team of three mechanical engineers and three electrical engineers. She treated her team well and they all accomplished their assigned tasks.

However, Barbara had the personal concept that her job was to find and solve problems. She moved through the world looking for potential problems. She had the reputation of being an engineer with a dark cloud over her head. Whenever Barbara attended a meeting, she would invariably be the person who brought up any possible problems. When she spoke, people cringed in anticipation of what negative factors she was likely to bring up. Her speech was riddled with words and phrases like *dire*, *difficult*, *major problem*, *failure*, *it won't work*, *we must know for sure*, and the like.

Over time, Barbara's reputation grew to the point that others did not want Barbara to attend their meetings. It became clear to her that she was being excluded from important meetings. Barbara figured out that it was probably because of her negative attitude and she was concerned that if she did not change her perspective and her behaviors, she would ultimately be let go from the company. See Figure 23.1.

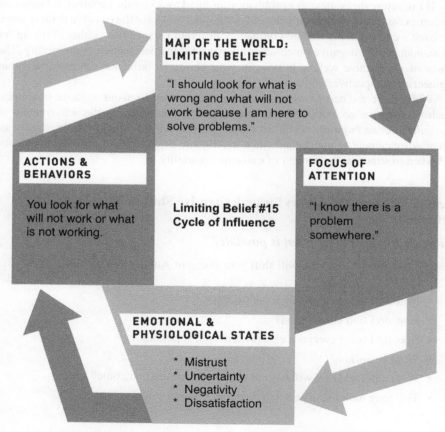

MAP OF THE WORLD: LIMITING BELIEF

"I should look for what is wrong and what will not work because I am here to solve problems."

ACTIONS & BEHAVIORS

You look for what will not work or what is not working.

Limiting Belief #15 Cycle of Influence

FOCUS OF ATTENTION

"I know there is a problem somewhere."

EMOTIONAL & PHYSIOLOGICAL STATES

* Mistrust
* Uncertainty
* Negativity
* Dissatisfaction

FIGURE 23.1. Career-Limiting Belief #15 Cycle of Influence.

Add Gem of Wisdom #15 to Your Current Map of the World

Shine a light: "I understand that looking for problems is different than looking for solutions. I now understand that the structure and context of a solution are as important to others as the solution itself."

If I make the statement that there is a problem that needs to be solved, your mind quickly looks for the problem. I am "pointing" your perspective toward the negative part of the situation, the problem area.

However, if I make the statement that there is something we want to accomplish and the question is how it can be accomplished, your mind automatically looks for the possible solution. I am "pointing" your perspective toward the positive part of the situation, the solution area.

If I structure the context as a problem, your mind looks for the problem. If I structure the context as a desired accomplishment, your mind looks for the possible achievement. An issue's context can structure completely different perspectives: either allowing for the avoidance of a negative outcome or allowing for the perspective of possibility. The power of perspective weighs heavily in your ability to influence others to see your engineering perspective.

While there are certain situations in which we want to avoid negative outcomes, much of what we accomplish in the engineering environment is the achievement of *possibility*. As an engineer, technical manager, or technologist, it is important to your career advancement to understand when to structure the context of problem avoidance and when to structure the context of outcome possibility.

Gem of Wisdom #15 Allows for an Expansive Shift in Your Focus of Attention

"How do I help achieve what is possible?"

Adding this gem to your map will shift your Focus of Attention to the following:

- How do I help achieve what is possible?
- How do I find the solution?
- How do I point everyone else toward what is possible?
- What is working?
- What can I add that will help us achieve the desired outcome?
- This may look like a problem but there is also a solution.

Gem #15 Produces Positive Physiological and Emotional States

The shift of focus will, in turn, generate new emotional and physiological states that allow the clouds to clear. Some of the new foci let you experience states that will move you toward the realm of the possible:

- Curiosity
- Flexibility
- Excitement
- Confidence

Gem of Wisdom #15 Allows for Career-Enhancing Actions and Behaviors

"I will approach solutions from the perspective of what is possible rather than always looking for the problems."

Your education has taught you how to be a problem solver. Now, your work environment would prefer that while you solved problems you also made new things possible. In other words, people do not want to only hear about the problems. Flip the structure, where problems lead to opportunities; then, the problems will look and feel less onerous. People want to see what is possible. Your influence will grow if you can consistently point people to what can be achieved instead of looking to avoid the landmines on the way.

By adding the Gem of Wisdom #15 you will expand your choice of behaviors from the positive perspective. Your new behaviors might include:

1. **You will ask more frequently, "What is the true desired outcome we want?"**
2. **You will more often direct the discussion in a positive direction.**
3. **You will be more likely to brainstorm with others rather than believing you have "the solution."**

Let's look at the above behaviors in more detail.

1. **You will ask more frequently, "What is the desired outcome we want?"**
   Very often, the reason that a negative perspective is taken is because engineers often decide what they think the outcome should be and then they look for all the reasons it may not be able to be achieved. As the engineer continues to look for what will not work, they creep farther and farther away from the true desired outcome. Therefore, in order to stay focused on the positive possibilities, keep focused on what is the true desired outcome. That means you may want to frequently "refresh" your mind and the discussion as to what the real goals and outcomes are. By reiterating and refocusing the discussion on the desired outcome, you can keep yourself and the discussion from veering off into the negative space.

2. **You will more often direct the discussion in a positive direction.** Once you begin to move through the world from a positive perspective, you will begin to notice when others are veering into the negative context. Feel free to redirect the meeting and the discussion toward the positive context. It is important and people will notice. You will be able to stop negative discussions in their tracks and redirect discussions toward finding solutions rather than looking for problems.

   To be sure, there will be times when the difference between finding solutions and looking for problems will be subtle, however the difference will be there. In my career, it has been clear that about 75% of my time is spent on the possible, the solution context, and only 25% of the time on looking for problems. Both are necessary, just not in equal measure.

3. **You will be more likely to brainstorm with others rather than believing you have "the solution."** One behavior that becomes evident when people are oriented toward the possible is that they are eager to brainstorm. Brainstorming does not exact much of a price, and so they are eager to engage in playing with ideas of what is possible. Even if their ideas will not work, they do not seem to care; they know that by focusing on what is the desired outcome, eventually the best ideas will come to the surface. Focusing on the possible will, much of the time, generate a workable solution.

Real World Example: Gem of Wisdom #15 in Action

Barbara was a good mechanical engineer. In fact, she had progressed to engineering manager of a team of three mechanical engineers and three electrical engineers. She treated her team well and they all accomplished their assigned tasks.

However, Barbara had the personal concept that her job was to find and solve problems. She moved through the world looking for problems to fix. She had the reputation of being an engineer with a dark cloud over her head. Whenever Barbara attended a meeting, she would invariably be the person who brought up the potential problems. Whenever Barbara spoke, people cringed in anticipation of what negative factors she might bring up.

Over time, Barbara's reputation grew to the point that others did not want her to attend their meetings. It became clear to Barbara that she was being excluded from important meetings. She figured out that it was probably because of her negative attitude and she was concerned that if she did not change her perspective and her behaviors, she would ultimately be let go from the company.

One day Barbara called me (yes, this is a true story) and she told me that she was being excluded from meetings because people were tired of her negative perspective. She was concerned about her future and she was desperate. She asked me to coach her, and so I helped her on several of the topics I have presented in this book, including this chapter.

Once Barbara had added several new Gems of Wisdom to her Map of the World and was comfortable with her new positive perspective, she decided to apply what she had learned to the world of her work environment.

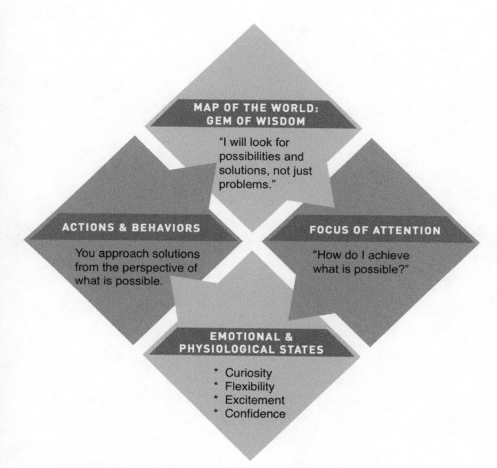

FIGURE 23.2. Career-Enhancing Gem of Wisdom #15 Cycle of Influence.

I did not hear from Barbara for several weeks. Then about four weeks after we completed our coaching, I received a phone call. She proceeded to tell me that things had completely changed for her. She was now being invited to meetings, even those where she wasn't really needed. When she asked the meeting leader why she was being invited to the meeting, Barbara was told that she contributed so much to the previous meeting's success that the meeting's leader wanted Barbara there each time.

Six months later, Barbara was promoted to director of engineering.

24

A Parting Letter From Steven

Most engineers try to avoid the "F" word and the "E" word (you know…Feelings and Emotions). One of the reasons we enjoy science, engineering, and technology so much is that emotions and feelings are generally absent. (This is a generalization, I know.) Our technical world is nice and predictable. There are no ambiguous responses or uncomfortable push-backs.

I have a simple response to this perspective: you are wrong.

Now, you might be able to dismiss the response that you are wrong if it were delivered from a psychologist or a therapist, for what do they know about the worlds of engineering, science, or technology? But you can't dismiss it from me. I'm an engineer and a scientist. I've been through what you are going through. The world of $F = ma$, of unambiguous answers, of non-emotional, unfeeling interactions is only one aspect of the "Big WORLD" within which you and I live, within which we all live.

As Hamlet said, "There are more things in heaven and earth, Horatio, than are dreamt of in your philosophy." And I would say to you that there are more things in life than the black and white of technology. There are people and emotions and feelings and relationships.

If you have a degree in engineering, or the sciences, or you are a capable technologist, then you have mastered some aspect of the technological world. However, if you want to succeed, long-term, in the world of technology, and in the world in general, then the emotional, the feeling, the non-technical aspect of your being must be mastered as

The Fully Integrated Engineer: Combining Technical Ability and Leadership Prowess, First Edition. Steven T. Cerri.
© 2016 The Institute of Electrical and Electronics Engineers, Inc. Published 2016 by John Wiley & Sons, Inc.

well, or at least effectively applied. And that is exactly why the Limiting Belief cycle and the Gem of Wisdom cycle both include a box titled, "Emotional and Physiological States." Your emotional and physiological states are as important to your long-term career success as are your technical knowledge and your behaviors.

This book is about helping you act in effective ways by adjusting your emotional and physiological states and this is done, in turn, by adjusting your Map of the World and your Focus of Attention.

I hope this book has helped you to see the strengths you have developed for the technological world and what strengths you must develop for the world in general. Because what is often missing for engineers, scientists, and technologists is the answer to this question: **"How do I best relate to the people with whom I work so that I can contribute my knowledge and expertise most effectively?"**

My goal has been to answer this question for you and to give you the tools to answer it for yourself on an ongoing basis. This book provides you with the means to assess what is not working in your career (and perhaps your life in general) and to make adjustments so you can turn it around.

If you find that there are certain chapters that are specifically applicable to you, focus on those. Not every chapter topic will resonate with you and your career to the same degree. So pick and choose what is most important to you, read and re-read those chapters, practice with the material, experiment. Unlike much in engineering, the material in this book does not provide you with perfect, right answers. There are only answers that are more or less effective.

Recently I learned how the Soviet Union developed the rocket engines that the United States is currently buying from Russia to launch US satellites into orbit and deliver astronauts and cargo to the International Space Station. Their philosophy, in the development of these highly efficient rocket engine assemblies, was this: "Build it, test it, fix it, test it…"

This is certainly not the approach used in the United States where we design each component and test each component until we are certain every component will work. It is only then that we put everything together as a system (i.e., the rocket engine) and test it as a unit. Unlike the Russians, we test our completely assembled rocket engines only when all components have been fully tested to provide a high probability that the system test will work. We abhor failures of any kind.

The Russians, on the other hand, built many versions of their "closed system" rocket engine and there were many, many failures on the way to the current, highly efficient, powerful, reliable, closed system rocket engines that the United States is purchasing from Russia. In fact, the United States engineers were initially in disbelief that the Russians could build a closed system rocket engine with such high efficiency because the US engineers had been unable to develop such an engine.

In a very real sense, this book is about just such a process for your professional development. There is no perfect path to success when it comes to the non-technical aspect of your professional development. It is indeed like this: "Try it, fix it, try it again, fix it again…"

Your career, and life in general, is a giant feedback loop of "try it, fix it, try it again…"

So leave behind the idea that there are right answers to everything. There are only right answers to equations and to software syntax and to other things that are technically based. But when it comes to your career, to your personal and professional growth, when it comes to achieving a long-term, happy career, it is indeed a "try it, fix it, try it..." process. So enjoy the ride.

I wish you all the best!

—Steven T. Cerri

And one more note: If you would like more information regarding training or coaching, or if you would like to contact me about speaking, or if you just want to make suggestions, contact me through my website: www.stevencerri.com or email me at steven@stevencerri.com.

Further Reading

S. Andreas and C. Faulkner, *NLP: The New Technology of Achievement*, New York, Quill William Morrow and Company, Inc., 1996.

R. Bandler and J. Grinder, *The Structure of Magic*, Palo Alto, CA, Science and Behavior Books, Inc., 1975.

R. Brodie, *Virus of the Mind: The New Science of the Meme*, Carlsbad, CA, Hay House, Inc., 1996.

S.T. Cerri, "The 5 Myths of Management," *Mechanical Engineering, The Magazine of ASME*, February 2009.

S.T. Cerri, "The balanced engineer: Essential ideas for career development," pgs. 47–58, Professional Activities Conference Proceedings, Technomic Publishing Co., Inc. 1998.

N. Chomsky, *Syntactic Structures*, 2nd ed., New York, Mouton de Gruyter, 2002.

R. B. Cialdini, *Influence: The Science and Practice*, 4th Edition, Boston, Allyn and Bacon, 2001.

G. Claxton, *Intelligence in the Flesh*, Yale University Press, New Haven and London, 2015.

R. Dilts, J. Grinder, R. Bandler, and J. DeLozier, *Neuro-Linguistic Programming: Volume 1, The Study of the Structure of Subjective Experience*, Meta Publications, Capitola, CA, 1980.

D. Eagleman, *Incognito: The Secret Lives of the Brain*, Pantheon Books, New York, 2011.

S. Knight, *NLP at Work: The Essence of Excellence, (People Skills for Professionals)*, 3rd ed., London, Nicholas Brealey Publishing, 2009.

G. Z. LaBorde, *Fine Tune Your Brain*, Syntony Publishing, Palo Alto, California, 1988.

G. Z. LaBorde, *Influencing With Integrity*, 2nd ed., Syntony Publishing, Palo Alto, CA, 1983.

M. Lindstrom, *Buy-Ology; Truth and Lies About Why We Buy*, Doubleday, New York, 2008.

A. Pentland, "To signal is human," *American Scientist*, vol. 98, no. 3, pp. 204–211, May-June, 2010.

J. Riggio, *The State of Perfection: Your Hidden Code to Unleashing Personal Mastery*, Smashwords Edition, 2012.

The Fully Integrated Engineer: Combining Technical Ability and Leadership Prowess, First Edition. Steven T. Cerri.
© 2016 The Institute of Electrical and Electronics Engineers, Inc. Published 2016 by John Wiley & Sons, Inc.

Biography of Steven T. Cerri

Steven T. Cerri is a facilitator, mentor/coach, speaker, and author. His specialty is in professional skills development for engineers, technical managers, and organizational leaders.

Since 1999, Cerri has helped thousands of technical professionals enhance their communication, management, and leadership skills through innovative training and facilitation, coaching, and published articles. As a sought-after speaker in the United States and internationally, he has presented at numerous industry association including AIAA (American Institute of Aeronautics & Astronautics), ASME (American Society of Mechanical Engineers), Rocky Mountain Workforce Development Association, and IEEE. He has worked with many of the top US aerospace corporations as well as many small and start-up organizations. As a former adjunct professor for the prestigious Technology Management Program at the University of California, Santa Barbara, he taught critical communication and business/entrepreneurship skills to graduate students.

Cerri's real world experience as an engineer, technical manager, organizational leader, and successful entrepreneur–coupled with his ability to understand and communicate with technical professionals–are what set him apart from other facilitators and mentors. He began his career as an aeronautical engineer employed at Rockwell International Corporation working on Skylab, Shuttle, Shuttle Tug, and Meteorological Satellite programs. Throughout his career, he has managed individuals and teams in both government and commercial organizations. He was part of a team that launched Infotec Development, a successful information technology (IT) firm focused on Department of Defense programs that was eventually bought by Pacer Systems, a British firm. Cerri has worked in the area of geophysical research and evaluation for the US Geological Service. He has been a program manager, director of corporate training, vice president of engineering, chief operations officer, and division general manager.

In every position he has held, it became apparent that he had a knack for training and coaching his employees to achieve extraordinary results. With this passion and expertise for teaching others, he eventually launched his own consulting and training organization to guide engineers and technical professionals to be as effective with people as they are with technology.

- Master of Business Administration, Pepperdine University
- Master of Science, Geophysics, University of Southern California
- Bachelor of Science, Aeronautical Engineering, California Polytechnic University
- Certified Master Practitioner of Neruo-Linguistic Programming
- Contributing Consultant/Speaker, PBS Television Series *Taking the Lead: The Management 2000 Revolution*
- Outstanding Professor Award, Technology Management Program, UC Santa Barbara
- Contributing author to the IEEE book: *The Balanced Engineer: Essential Ideas for Career Development*
- International Who's Who of Professional Management

Steven T. Cerri is founder of STCerri International, an international facilitation/training, consulting, and mentoring/coaching company. Contact Steven T. Cerri / STCerri International at 231 Market Place, Suite 320, San Ramon, CA 94583 Office 925-735-9500. For information regarding facilitation/training or speaking, contact Cerri at:

Email: steven@stevencerri.com
Website: http://www.stevencerri.com

For information regarding mentoring/coaching or speaking, contact Cerri at:

Email: steven@acementoring.com
Website: http://www.acementoring.com

Index

The Fully Integrated Engineer: Combining Technical Ability and Leadership Prowess, First Edition. Steven T. Cerri.
© 2016 The Institute of Electrical and Electronics Engineers, Inc. Published 2016 by John Wiley & Sons, Inc.

Books in the
IEEE PCS PROFESSIONAL ENGINEERING COMMUNICATION SERIES

Sponsored by IEEE Professional Communication Society

Series Editor: Traci Nathans-Kelly

This series from IEEE's Professional Communication Society addresses professional communication elements, techniques, concerns, and issues. Created for engineers, technicians, academic administration/faculty, students, and technical communicators in related industries, this series meets a need for a targeted set of materials that focus on very real, daily, on-site communication needs. Using examples and expertise gleaned from engineers and their colleagues, this series aims to produce practical resources for today's professionals and pre-professionals.

Information Overload: An International Challenge for Professional Engineers and Technical Communicators · Judith B. Strother, Jan M. Ulijn, and Zohra Fazal

Negotiating Cultural Encounters: Narrating Intercultural Engineering and Technical Communication · Han Yu and Gerald Savage

Slide Rules: Design, Build, and Archive Presentations in the Engineering and Technical Fields · Traci Nathans-Kelly and Christine G. Nicometo

A Scientific Approach to Writing for Engineers & Scientists · Robert E. Berger

Engineer Your Own Success: 7 Key Elements to Creating an Extraordinary Engineering Career · Anthony Fasano

International Virtual Teams: Engineering Global Success · Pam Estes Brewer

Communication Practices in Engineering, Manufacturing, and Research for Food and Water Safety · David Wright

Teaching and Training For Global Engineering: Perspectives On Culture And Professional Communication Practices · Kirk St.Amant and Madelyn Flammia

The Fully Integrated Engineer: Combining Technical Ability and Leadership Prowess · Steven Cerri

Printed and bound by CPI Group (UK) Ltd, Croydon, CR0 4YY

16/04/2025

14658456-0004